An American's Grand Slam

An American's Grand Slam

A True Adventurer's Unlikely Journey

Ryan Waters and

Hudson Lindenberger

ESSEX, CONNECTICUT

FALCONGUIDES®

An imprint of Globe Pequot, the trade division of The Rowman & Littlefield Publishing Group, Inc.
4501 Forbes Blvd., Ste. 200
Lanham, MD 20706
www.rowman.com

Distributed by NATIONAL BOOK NETWORK

British Library Cataloguing in Publication Information Available

Library of Congress Cataloging-in-Publication Data
Names: Waters, Ryan, 1973– author. | Lindenberger, Hudson, author.
Title: An American's grand slam : a true adventurer's unlikely journey / Ryan Waters and Hudson Lindenberger.
Description: Guilford, Connecticut : Falcon Guides, 2022.
Identifiers: LCCN 2022004212 (print) | LCCN 2022004213 (ebook) | ISBN 9781493060054 (paperback) | ISBN 9781493060061 (epub)
Subjects: LCSH: Waters, Ryan, 1973– | Mountaineers—United States—Biography.
Classification: LCC GV199.92.W384 A3 2022 (print) | LCC GV199.92.W384 (ebook) | DDC 796.522092 [B]—dc23/eng/20220406
LC record available at https://lccn.loc.gov/2022004212
LC ebook record available at https://lccn.loc.gov/2022004213

CONTENTS

Acknowledgments

Looking back, my personal journey through the True Adventurers Grand Slam includes a mix of luck, perseverance, and sacrifice, but most of all the incredible support I was fortunate to receive from many. Without guidance from family, friends, and colleagues, and random encounters along the way, it would have been impossible to have success on these challenging endeavors, or even the opportunity to take part in them.

Thank you most of all to my supportive family for helping me out along the way: My mother, Kathy, and father, Alan, whose unconditional love cannot be replaced; when I decided to leave a career and pursue a dream in the outdoors, they chose to support that path. My brother Tate, a role model and teacher in many ways, who is always there no matter what. My wonderful aunts JoJo and Gayle, my uncle Jimmy, Melody, Randy, Megan, Torrey, Brandon, and their families, as well as our extended family in Georgia, Texas, and Illinois.

A special gratitude and many thanks for being incredible partners on the ice and beyond go to Cecilie Skog and Eric Larsen.

Hudson Lindenberger, who not only challenged me on the tennis court but made sense of a long, world-circling narrative. He is the reason I was able to put pen to paper and have my memories tell my story.

I have been lucky to have many great friendships along the way, each in the different stages of life detailed in this story: great high school and college friends who remain lifelong brothers: John Raffa, Kevin Zier, Chase Connor, David Gauch, Matthew Kamler, Brad Warbington, Andy Sandlin, Rob Maczuga, and many more teammates and fraternity brothers and friends from the Southeast.

I have had many mountaineering and climbing partners or inspirational figures in my life whom I am grateful to, including but not limited to John Reiboldt, Dave Elmore, Tomas Ceppi, Doug Sandok, Diego and Lucila Magaldi, Tashi Sherpa, Chhering Dorjee Sherpa, Russell Brice, and Tshering Sherpa for the many Himalayan journeys.

Thank you to Antarctic Logistics and Expeditions, Kenn Borek Air, Himalayan Trailblazers, Kili Expeditions and Safaris, Grajales Expeditions, Indonesia Explorer, Lela Peak Expeditions, Tom and Tina Sjogren, Explorersweb, Nikoli Savin, Phil Crampton, Dan Mazur, Peter Whittaker, North Carolina Outward Bound School, Brady Robinson, Ted Alexander, Katherine Homes, Tara Skredynski, Maria Hennessey, Bjørn Sekkesæter, Faustin, Ignas, and Leon Meela, Katrina Follows, Lars Ebbesen, Marc De Keyser, Paul Adams, Scott Kress, Silje Hanum Padøy, and Linn Kathrine Yttervik.

To the Bae family, Cooper family, and Hanson family.

Though she arrived in my life after the North Pole and thus the Grand Slam, Lore Vázquez Morton, who has been such an amazing, understanding, patient, and supportive partner. She and Sofia are simply the best.

Ryan Waters

From the first time I met Ryan Waters, through our mutual friend, polar explorer Eric Larsen, I was fascinated by his story of a southern boy much like myself falling in love with the wilderness. But, while I chose to follow a much more contemporary, well-worn path, Ryan decided to head out into the wilds following in the footsteps of so many famous explorers and adventurers that we both grew up reading stories about. To be able to help him tell his story was both a privilege and a pleasure.

Hudson Lindenberger

Prologue: Crying in My Goggles

"I should write a country song called 'crying in my goggles,'" I mumbled to my expedition partner, Eric Larsen, through cracked lips. Fighting back the tears brought on by exhaustion, frustration, and the 480 nautical miles of Arctic Ocean sea ice we had struggled across over the last fifty-two days since we had left the solid soil of Canada, I was wrung out. With just six nautical miles left to reach the North Pole, it was the only phrase I could think to utter after a desperate, hour-long block of time navigating out front for our small team of two. The clock was ticking, and every minute counted. The ice was continually moving underfoot. Every moment we were not moving toward our goal, I worried that all the effort we had put in could result in failure. This starts to affect your thoughts and emotions, bringing negative thoughts that can end a trip.

After endless days of dangerously little sleep, hopeless visibility, and exhaustion the like of which I had never experienced, I finally showed the first outward emotional crack. The battle with the elements, drifting ice, polar bears, and seemingly every other force in the world that appeared to be conspiring against us was taking its toll. Our mental strength and fortitude as a team and as individuals were waning with every disappointing setback, however minor they might have been.

Everything hinged on us making it there. We were attempting something that fewer than forty-five people had ever done: an unsupported ski expedition to the North Pole. For the last fifty days, it had been just the two of us dragging all our supplies across a broken and battered landscape that was constantly changing. We had made significant commitments—both personal and professional—to be here, and the idea of failing this close to our goal weighed heavily on us.

Eric Larsen also was, like myself, a professional adventurer. His background was built on highly challenging polar skiing expeditions to some of the most remote locations on the planet. He had skied twice before to the North Pole on supported trips, where the team received resupplies of food and fuel dropped in caches along the way. Eric also had become the first person in history to climb Mount Everest and ski to the North and South Poles via full-length trips in a single year.

Our personal and professional commitments basically hinged on finishing this unsupported ski expedition from Cape Discovery (a geographic feature more than an actual place), located on Canada's far north reaches, to the North Pole. In a sense, the North Pole isn't really a place either. There is nothing there, just a geographic landmark, albeit a magical landmark on the constantly changing ice map. This point marks the top of the earth with floating sea ice and nothing else.

To complete an unsupported, full-length ski expedition to the North Pole means leaving land with all the supplies needed to make the 480-nautical-mile journey over arguably the most demanding terrain on the planet. It's often referred to as the most challenging type of expedition to pull off anywhere in the world. No outside help. No resupplies. No assistance of any sort. Our sleds had each weighed 320 pounds when we skied away from the nonexistent ice runway at Cape Discovery, where the ski-equipped Twin Otter aircraft had dropped us and bid us farewell.

With huge sums of money, sponsors, relationships, and family commitments at stake, we had the additional pressure to film our expedition for Discovery Channel/Animal Planet, which had come on as a major sponsor. A trek to the North Pole is arduous to accomplish under any circumstances. But our trip took on an added level of complexity due to the decision to film it. We had to keep batteries charged, constantly stop to set up cameras, and debate the pros and cons of wasting valuable time skiing through a shot and then going back to retrieve the movie camera. It had greatly contributed to our stress level.

The Arctic Ocean is a constantly shifting maze of floating ice. The difficulty of travel in that environment is magnified by the extreme cold that is ever present. Considering our expedition's unsupported nature, we were forced to travel with extremely heavy sleds that carried all the supplies needed for a planned journey no longer than fifty-five days. The Arctic ice is affected by seasonal temperatures, ocean currents, and wind. It varies in thickness from open water to a thin veneer of flexible ice just millimeters thick to sheets ten feet thick. Regardless, it is always on the move, and blocks, or pans, of ice constantly shift and slowly crash into each other, creating pressure ridges of ice piled up as high as twelve feet.

To travel with a 300-plus-pound sled across that surface is back-breaking work. Constantly navigating and trying to find a feasible way forward is taxing. In temperatures as low as minus 58 degrees F, seemingly never-ending wind, and lurking polar bears, the slightest mistake can be deadly.

We were so close to completing our objective after skiing, snowshoeing, and even swimming the frigid Arctic seawater in survival suits for 480 nautical miles. But a never-ending series of obstacles kept tearing at our thin veil of optimism, threatening to destroy it. Polar ski travel is a combination of many skills, the most important being the ability to follow a compass bearing. Ever since humans first laid a set of latitude and longitude lines across the globe to assist in maritime navigation, we have been able to locate ourselves with a group of coordinates. In the past, before the modern-day Global Positioning System (GPS) did all the work, explorers and sailors used a device called a sextant. Through a complicated series of steps to measure the horizon in relation to stars and sun, time of year, and time of day, one could locate themselves on the map via their coordinates and thus figure out what compass bearing they should be traveling to reach another set of coordinates.

GPS has made the process so much simpler. Using satellites to pinpoint your location, you plug in the coordinates you want to reach. The device can then calculate a compass bearing that you should follow to reach your destination. On a polar ski expedition, having a good compass bearing to follow is crucial when whiteouts make it impossible to distinguish the difference between the snow you are skiing on and the air surrounding you. It's like traveling in a bowl of smoke; everything is upside down, and the only thing you can focus on is your compass or the person directly in front of you leading the way. I had been skiing in the lead, navigating for the last several hours, and the visibility was down to about sixteen feet due to the dusty snow swirling around us. I had to constantly keep one eye on my compass, following its bearing toward 90 degrees north to the top of the world. The problem was that after so many days on the ice with so little sleep, coupled with so much physical and mental exertion, we were shot. It was difficult to make any progress.

When there is no visibility, you just move forward in a direction that feels three-dimensional. Nothing really makes sense. Skiing through a maze of looming chunks of ice that forced us to change direction, filled with smaller blocks of ice that kept hooking our ski tips, tripping us up, I was disheartened. In the whiteout conditions, we'd often ski right into a large block of ice before we even knew it was there. Or we'd ski forward horizontally just fine for a while, then realize our ski tips had gone nearly vertical after running into an elevated pressure ridge. Worse would be a sudden fall through a lead or crack in the ice into the Arctic Ocean. Wearing clothes soaked in near-freezing water while standing in an ambient air temperature of minus 22 degrees F would put an instant stop to any forward progress, if you could manage to get out of the water at all.

After swapping leads over the course of six hours, for the first time on the trip I felt wholly finished, physically and mentally. My steel reserve finally broke and allowed a dangerous thought to enter my mind: Maybe we were not going to make it.

As another hour wound down, this time with me leading in the muck, I heard Eric ski up behind me. He was equally frustrated, depressed, and overly tired. I began to explain that I couldn't see anything, and every time I thought the surface would open up and we'd get a break, it just got worse. "I know, man, I'm sorry," Eric said to me with a sad crack in his voice, intimately knowing the feeling I was going through. I cried for the first time that I could remember.

How do you continue on when you feel broken? Even though we were so close to our goal, I felt like quitting. The last fifty-two days did not matter. It did not matter to me that we had begged and cajoled the flight company via satellite phone to give us an extra two days to get to the Pole—even though they were wary about their ability to pluck us off the rapidly changing ice pack and there was a chance we might be stranded. I thought maybe we should just give up and call them in to get us. It would not be the first time I had failed at a major expedition objective. A valiant effort of *almost* reaching the North Pole, for what might realistically be the last time anyone could accomplish the feat because of global warming, should still count for something.

In my youth, wandering the mountain streams and relatively forgiving mountainous terrain of northern Georgia, did I ever in my wildest dreams foresee such a major outdoor accomplishment within my grasp? The North Pole trip is a dream trip in itself, but I was also just six nautical miles away from becoming the first American to complete what is known as the "True Adventurers Grand Slam," which comprises climbing the Seven Summits (the highest mountain on each continent) and skiing unsupported (no resupplies or outside help) and unassisted (no mechanical, wind, or guide help) on full-length ski expeditions to both Poles.

I drew upon an internal mental strength and commitment that I had gained over fourteen years of climbing and polar expeditions worldwide. I had learned the stinging lessons of turning back short of major mountain summits. I was sure I could somehow get over failing here, but I had made an internal pact with myself and carried not only a goal but a commitment that no matter what happened, I would not give up on the Arctic Ocean.

I looked at Eric through my tears; they were hidden behind my goggles, but I knew he knew they were there. He had had his own moments on this expedition when everything seemed hopeless too. He reached into his pocket and fished out a piece of salami and cheese, our go-to ration on this trip, and tossed it to me. I unwrapped it and took a bite, and just focused for a moment on chewing the half-frozen ration. I gazed at the desolate wasteland, and my mind wandered to another time when things seemed hopeless, when I did not know if I could go on.

Undertaking the challenge of skiing to the North Pole unsupported is not some rash decision. Adventurers need years of experience, not only in polar environments but also in the outdoors in general. There are so many skills that one must have in their quiver. With thousands of tiny details all making up a larger goal, it is imperative that a team can troubleshoot and resurrect suddenly dormant stoves and damaged ski gear, administer first aid when needed, be able to navigate in all kinds of conditions, and continually make judgment calls while assessing current situations that are constantly changing. There are so many obstacles to overcome each day, it can be overwhelming, and only the most seasoned outdoor people can draw upon their days in similar situations to fix problems.

You don't get that kind of experience overnight. For me, it was a thirteen-year journey to get to the Arctic Ocean. I had spent countless field days in charge of clients in Patagonia's mountains and the Andes of South America, guided people on mountains on every continent, led around fifteen Himalayan expeditions, and skied across Greenland and Antarctica. Each of these experiences was an integral piece of the puzzle in my quest for the North Pole. Not all were successful. In fact, the failures in my past often taught me the most valuable lessons in the outdoors and helped me gain practical experience and judgment. One of the most important lessons was to know when to turn around, which I learned in the most unforgiving and dangerous mountain range on the planet.

KARAKORAM RANGE, PAKISTAN, 2006

The four of us had been climbing for roughly six hours up the treacherous slopes of K2, the second-highest peak on the planet. Since we left Camp Three at 23,700 feet, we had been swapping positions in the front, taking turns kicking steps for the others to follow ever higher. This is the worst position to be in when climbing, especially on the 50-degree slope we were traversing. The snow came up to our knees with each step, making the effort to kick a step to stand on even more exhausting than it usually was. With sixty-six-pound packs riding on our back, none of us could stay up front long before exhaustion kicked in. When the man behind you took the lead, and you could fall to the back of the line and follow the freshly blazed trail, you were immensely grateful.

We were trying to pioneer the route from Camp Three at 23,622 feet upward to Camp Four, located at 25,080 feet on the Abruzzi Shoulder. This was in 2006, back in the day when K2 was still relegated to mountaineers from around the world, all pitching in from different teams to make the route in a collective effort. All the rope fixing was done in a patchwork assembly of agreed-upon terms. Which team would put in how much rope and who would push the route upward was decided at unbearably long meetings in unheated tents at base camp.

Although I had just finished climbing two 8,000-meter, or 26,247-foot, mountains within the previous month and a half—Cho Oyu at 26,906 feet, the sixth-highest mountain in the world, located in Tibet; and K2's towering neighbor, Broad Peak at 26,401 feet, the twelfth-highest mountain—climbing another of the fourteen mountains in the world over 8,000 meters seemed like a perfectly normal course of action. I was in my early thirties with no real commitment to speak of other than a storage unit in Boulder, Colorado. I was armed with an insatiable thirst for climbing the world's highest peaks in the most incredible mountain ranges. Over the last month in the Karakoram, I had spent time working with my team and climbers from other international expeditions to fix ropes and stock successively higher camps on the Abruzzi Ridge route of the infamous K2, a place that climbers call the "Savage Mountain" for its relatively high failure and death rate.

As one of the more complex and dangerous mountains globally, summiting K2 is highly dependent on the weather and high alpine conditions. All the teams attempting to summit must work together to successfully prepare a pathway upward. But even if the ropes are set and steps cut, success is not guaranteed. Often a season will end with no successful summits.

I was part of a small team that worked feverishly to put in the route to Camp Four. The group consisted of myself, Ger McDonnell and Mick Murphy from Ireland, and Wilco Van Rooijen of the Netherlands. Since we had spent the last month climbing nearby Broad Peak, the lines were already laid to Camp Two by the time we arrived. This allowed us to spend a few weeks getting our own teams prepared by hauling supplies up to the lower camps.

Knowing that a small weather window was forecast to open soon, which would allow attempts on the summit, all the teams realized that the final ropes had to get placed on the route to Camp Four, the last high camp before the summit. Since we were the new guys to camp, we drew the short straw. We were okay with heading higher, loaded down with ropes, to help the collective on the mountain. Plus, we would get to set the ropes to the summit after a night at Camp Four.

As we struggled upward, saddled with huge loads of our own equipment and heavy coils of rope for fixing lines above Camp Three, we realized something was wrong. The other teams that were supposed to be helping us had turned around somewhere above Camp Two the previous day. There would be no help. Instead, the four of us carried the hopes of all the teams below on our backs. If we did not get the ropes fixed and the route laid, the fragile weather window might be missed, as others would have to ascend to finish what we could not complete. The pressure was immense; we did not want to let everyone down.

We were just below the shoulder, close to cresting out and reaching the Camp Four location but mired in waist-deep snow. Beat down by our heavy loads and the difficult route-finding, we started to question our ability to complete the task. I had already amassed a little bit of experience and judgment by this point in my climbing career, having climbed Everest and other major peaks in the Himalayas and other mountain ranges. A voice in my head began to tell me, "This probably isn't your time on K2." I was exhausted from the two recent expeditions to the summit of Cho Oyu and Broad Peak. Still, as a serious mountaineer, so close to Camp Four on K2, it was hard to admit that an extremely long and dangerous summit day just over the horizon might not be so safe.

As we slogged ever higher, each of us battling our own inner demons and voices, something slowly became clear to the four of us: We were probably off course. Looking around, we realized we were likely off the planned route and instead in a very tenuous spot that was prime for avalanches. We started to move in the direction we were sure would put us back in safer conditions. Let me tell you, being high in the Himalayas, clinging to the side of a mountain in a dangerous spot is not somewhere you want to be. It provided us with a boost of energy as we worked to remedy our situation. But, just as quickly, the high, thin air started slowing our pace again, and we began swapping out positions in the lead more frequently. The adrenaline high dissipated, and things got even more challenging.

Eventually, at a break, I told my teammates that I was done. I did not have enough energy to stay at the altitude of Camp Four and help carry and fix ropes to the summit. With the weight of the situation filling the cold air between us, we debated our next course of action. Should we continue on or turn back? Eventually, all agreed that we should go back down to Camp Three and reassess our individual and team plans. After a long night full of thought and contemplation, not made any easier by the fact that we were four tired climbers jammed into a tilted, uneven three-person tent, we decided to head back down to base camp the following day. I questioned the decision. After all the work it took to get to this spot, was it in vain?

I got the definitive answer from the mountain gods that this was not my time to reach the summit of K2 soon. That morning, as I rappelled down the fixed line toward Camp Two, concentrating on the terrain below me, I heard the familiar, high-pitched whine of a falling rock coming from above. In a split second, it crashed into my left knee. I was stunned. I immediately thought my knee was broken, and my mind automatically went into triage mode. How was I going to get myself down the thousands of vertical feet to advanced base camp? I kneeled over and breathed, slowly moving my leg; it was excruciating, but I could tell it was not broken, though a severe bruise would follow. That was the final sign I needed. It was time to go. I could come back another time; the mountain would always be here.

As the expedition leader, I made the difficult call to officially end our trip. The most realistic summit push had fallen short for us. In my opinion, we were facing dangerous late-season conditions and time constraints. I had failed. It was a tough pill to swallow. K2 had proved too challenging that season. Maybe because of trying to climb three 8,000-meter peaks in a row, I had exhausted my body.

Once we got to base camp, I talked quite a lot with Ger, Wilco, and Mick, who were thinking about staying for one more shot at a summit push. They discussed the idea with our liaison officer and were able to switch places onto another climbing permit. This allowed a patchwork of climbers from various teams a chance to spend more time there and give it another crack.

The rest of our group spent a few days in the K2 base camp, organizing gear and making plans for the trek out. It would be an arduous walk over rigorous terrain for several days to reach a basic road. My job was to work with our logistics organizer from Pakistan to arrange porters to assist in the load carries of personal and group gear. I briefed the group on the route we would trek over the next few days. We had to go over the Gondogoro Pass and then descend into the small village known as Hushe, located at the extreme end of a remote valley in the Ghangche District. Hushe was our exit point, where we would meet four-wheel-drive vehicles prearranged to return the group back to Skardu, the larger city where most Karakoram expeditions begin and end.

Our principal high-altitude Pakistani porter for the expedition was named Tashe. He was a strong and humble young man who was very proud. He looked forward to showing us his home village of Hushe, where many of the older males have grown accustomed to working as cooks and porters for climbing expeditions. We made the high, snowy traverse of the Gondogoro Pass, which at an elevation of 18,323 feet feels like climbing another mountain, and slept for the night in our mountain tents. Another extremely long and hot day hiking down into the rocky valley's lower elevations brought us to the village.

Tashe invited us into his home. He was eager to show us his simple but neat room and introduce us to his family. We drank tea, with water heated over an open fire, on the dirt kitchen floor. His mother proudly displayed her cooking pots and utensils on the wall of the dimly lit room. She offered crackers and soup to the strange foreigners that had assembled in her kitchen. I realized there are other experiences on expeditions that are just as meaningful as a summit. The relationships you build, the starkly different cultures you encounter, and the simple kindness of warm tea stick in your mind long after you get home.

Upon reaching Skardu, the closest real town to the great Karakoram mountains, I settled into our lodge and finally began to relax and unwind a bit. Three of our expedition team members had decided to stay on and give the summit of K2 one last-ditch effort. I got word that while climbing back up to Camp Two, Ger had been hit in the head by a falling rock.

His climbing helmet was the only thing that saved his life, but reportedly he was in very bad shape.

I was switched back on.

Even though the guys were on their own, I still felt a part of their effort in some small way. Our local logistics operator had dispatched a military helicopter to airlift Ger out of base camp back to Skardu for treatment. More bad news followed with the news that a Russian team trying for the summit triggered an avalanche, killing several of their team members. I finally processed my personal decision to turn around and discovered it was the right one for me at the time. This was a fundamental building block in my experience as a mountain climber.

That expedition led to great friendships that would fuel emails and marathon Skype sessions about big dreams on other mountains and eventually another planned attempt at K2. This was the beginning of a standard set of circular paths that developed in my world of adventure. These circles would bring familiar people and themes into my personal life and professional career. Sadly, I would lose some of those same friends to K2 in a 2008 tragedy that took eleven lives. It was one of the deadliest single days in mountaineering history and an expedition that I was supposed to be on.

I was on one of the climbing permits for K2 in the summer of 2008. I was offered a spot with Ger and Wilco's team, one I had climbed with before and liked, but I declined the offer. I decided to go with a small American team instead. I wanted the intimacy that a smaller team provided. I knew all the teams would be helping each other to climb the mountain, and so it did not make too much difference which permit I was actually on. I was just eager to get back on the slopes and give the mountain another shot. I also knew that a Norwegian climbing and polar superstar friend I had met in 2007 named Cecilie Skog would be there. She also had been planning to go back to K2 that summer. (After the season was over, I found an email from her where she said, "You should go to K2. I hear it is going to be a great summer.") Little did either of us know then what was about to happen on the mountain that year. Of course, there was no way for anyone to know what conditions would be like so far ahead.

I was already signed on to guide Everest in the spring of 2008. I figured it would be a great way to get in shape for K2. All I would require was some downtime between the two expeditions, and I would be ready for a strong climb in Pakistan again.

On our Everest summit evening late in May 2008, I had an issue with the oxygen regulator that sends the vital air from the bottle to the oxygen mask. At the time, we were still using the older Piosk regulators, which were standard and reasonably reliable. However, every now and again, people would have an issue with them freezing up. This was why we always carried spares on the summit morning.

I was at the Balcony of Everest, located at around 27,560 feet. When I changed my bottle for a new cylinder, I realized the air was not getting through the iced-up regulator. My Sherpa team, which had our spares, was about forty minutes ahead of me, except for our Sirdar, or head climbing Sherpa, who was behind me with one of our clients. I had been trying to stay in the middle of the team, but the last client, along with our Sirdar, had turned back. So I climbed without oxygen for about thirty minutes, trying to catch the rest of my team at a break. But the clients were moving quickly, so the Sherpas with the spare regulators were far ahead. I was climbing without oxygen after having used it for several hours—a bad idea at the best of times. The result was that I got freezing feet, and unknown to me, I had developed frostbite on my big toe.

I was on the radio with my Sherpa climbing staff up ahead. Everyone on the team was doing very well and climbing fast. They were about to summit and turn back. There was no way I would catch them—especially switching from using oxygen to not using it, which can be dangerous at high altitudes. Since we had one guide for every client and they were moving quickly, I felt confident that I could descend and be a support person for the team. I descended to Camp Four to wait for them to arrive safely back down.

That afternoon, my team had either already started down with Sherpas or were safely back in the tents at Camp Four. So I figured I might as well head back up that evening to nab the summit. With a new regulator and some spare oxygen left over for an emergency, I started up again that night by myself. I felt surprisingly strong all the way and reached the summit in a pretty fast time. However, I believe the damage of climbing earlier in the day without supplemental oxygen had taken a toll without me realizing it, and the cold toe had already done its damage. When I got back to the tent at Camp Four, I was by myself. I was drained and feeling some serious effects from staying so long at altitude. I pulled off my boots to reveal a small bubble developing on my big toe's skin. I quickly made a pot of hot water and submerged my toes, trying to rewarm them before getting into the sleeping bag for much-needed sleep.

The descent the next day was terrible. I had to pack up all the remaining gear and head down with a pretty heavy backpack. I knew our team was doing well and on its way from Camp Two back to base camp. I knew the clients were in good hands with our staff, so that was a relief. My feet were hurting, and I felt miserable from what I later learned was the onset of pulmonary edema. I carried my personal gear and part of the group's gear back down from Camp Four to Camp Two, a long downhill slog. When I finally got close, I had to call a teammate on the radio to bring me up some more oxygen. I spent a long night consumed with coughing fits to expel the liquid trying to invade my lungs. But the next morning, I felt much better. So I started down to base camp and arrived with no issues. In the end, this was yet another learning experience of what not to do, another entry in my mental journal of experiences to draw from. I have gone on to climb and guide Everest and many other 8,000-meter mountains numerous times since and have never again had cold or altitude issues.

Once I got back to Kathmandu after the successful climb on Everest, I was in great shape, but my toe had begun to turn funny colors. I had to call my K2 team and tell them I was out for this season. Little did I know how fortuitous that frostbitten toe turned out to be.

If I had gone to K2, I would have been right there with the climbers who were killed or trapped high on K2's unforgiving slopes in one of the worst mountaineering disasters in recent history. Perhaps one who saw the serac release right above the infamous bottleneck below the peak's summit and result in chaos. Several more avalanches followed soon after. Eleven climbers lost their lives on the mountain. My North Pole partner, Eric, likes to say that I am the luckiest unlucky guy in the world.

The events of that tragedy, the recurring circles of the Savage Mountain, and this wild and crazy adventure life would eventually lead me to strap skis on my feet and discover that there are more adventures to be had—this time on the horizontal ice of the polar regions. Accustomed to going high, this mountaineer would try to go far: to ski across Antarctica and eventually end up just six nautical miles from the North Pole, crying in his goggles.

CHAPTER ONE

What, Me Grow Up?

THERE ARE TIMES WHEN I AM GUIDING CLIENTS ON A TRIP IN SOME faraway landscape or remote mountain location around the world when I have a sudden, powerful remembrance of being a teenager. Suddenly my imagination takes me back there, to the days of wondering what I would someday do for work and how I could make a living in the outdoors. Even at a young age, I felt such a draw to natural places that, deep down, I knew I needed to find a way to have a career that would allow me to be outside.

My job is filled with moments of sublime beauty. Moments that are burned into my memories. The white teeth shining from the dark and dusty faces of the colorful gauchos that rode by on their towering horses as I hiked toward a summit in the Argentinian highlands. The sweet water sipped from a stream trickling over moss coated rocks in a nameless valley in Nepal. Those things stick with you.

I have been lucky to share so many amazing experiences with people in some of the strangest corners of the planet. I had many close calls, situations that could have turned out horribly bad for me but didn't. Still, so many more of my memories are of incredible highs, individual and group achievements. I have trekked, climbed, skied, and sailed my way around this planet of ours, yet still the people and places intrigue me to no end.

After guiding trips for nearly twenty years now, some things have become routine. It is inevitable, no matter what your profession is. I am simply fortunate that my chosen path, after all these years, still has the power to stop me in my tracks to take in my surroundings. No matter the challenges, I can always sit on a large boulder in the Karakoram Valley of Pakistan, or on my expedition sled in the vast white expanse of Antarctica, and think, holy shit, this is the best job in the world.

I know that I have an authentic connection to natural places. Being in the outdoors has become my default religion. Often, while my clients diligently purify their drinking bottles with iodine tablets, having read one too many outdoor articles about how everything needs to be treated, I sneak a drink straight from the source and sit quietly. Those moments of peace amid an expedition are something that I savor, and remind me how far I have come from my childhood in Georgia.

My close friends and I grew up exploring the hills at the southern end of one of the earth's oldest chain of mountains, the Appalachian Mountains. At one time higher than the Himalayas, the Appalachians perhaps now conjure up visions of a toothless hillbilly playing the banjo. Still, I found them intriguing, with pockets of dense forest, beautiful rivers, and rocky granite crags to climb. Going on camping trips with heavy tin cans of baked beans and bacon dutifully packed away in our external frame packs, we would journey into what we at the time considered the extreme outdoors.

To this day, I often joke with friends from outside the region I grew up in that I am not to blame for my shortcomings. What did they expect from a good old boy from the South? It's easy to play on the common stereotypes associated with that part of the world. The reality is that I grew up in a close-knit family that provided a loving and comfortable environment that nurtured my interests. Marietta, Georgia, was a town caught in a time of transition. Pockets of old Atlanta money and numerous Civil War statues dotted the landscape. Still, it was far enough away from the metropolis (twenty miles) to feel like another world. It was ideally situated with forests and creeks and plenty of space for a young boy to roam. Yet it had high-quality schools and a beautiful heart.

There was a natural progression for most boys where I grew up. As youths, we would run around in the woods in camouflage outfits imitating characters from movies like *Platoon* or *Rambo*. That led to an interest in hunting and eventually into backpacking. When we finally were old enough to notice, all this led to an excuse to get girls and beer out to a friend's piece of country land to go camping. Our interests evolved with age, but the underlying theme always revolved around just being outside in some capacity.

When I was about thirteen years old, a friend of mine let me ride his new dirt bike on the trails cut through the kudzu-laden hills at the back of our neighborhood alongside Soap Creek. A divine revelation occurred that day, and I believed that my life's work now lay in the hands of the motocross gods. Every moment was spent devising a way to get my hands on a motorcycle of my own, and I was determined to make the dream a reality. I approached my parents with the idea of purchasing an 80cc Honda motocross bike. They supported the idea but came up with the plan that if I could pay for half the bike, they would take care of the other half. So I set about saving every penny to try to cobble together enough funds to make good on our contract. That following summer, as I was about to turn fourteen years old, I got a job at a local tree and flower shop, watering the plants and helping load cars in the humid summer heat. I loved it; I actually enjoyed learning about the different plants I was working with. I knew that each paycheck, as meager as they were, was getting me closer to my goal of a new Honda CR 80!

With the end of summer drawing to a close and my eighth-grade year in middle school quickly approaching, I knew I would come up just short on my half of the funding. I had worked very hard to save enough money, and my parents knew it. I figured it would take me another year to make enough money to pay my half and sadly began to accept the fact that I would not reach my goal. One day, when I came home from the summer two-a-day football practices that had started, I saw my parents sitting in the gazebo in our backyard with a funny grin on their faces. Tired and ready for rest, I approached them, not in the best mood. They told me to turn around. Leaned up against a tree was my brand-new motorcycle. They had decided to make up the difference in our half and half agreement and purchased the lion's share of my newfound passion. I literally slept next to it that night in our basement and then proceeded to live and breathe motocross.

I learned how to work on my bike, made a tool station in our basement, and rode with friends at the horse farms around our neighborhood almost every day. It was a magical time, so much so that I got a job at the Honda dealership and worked part-time in the parts department the following summer. I was in motorcycle heaven. To this day it is still a passion of mine, though I have not owned one in many years. It took me turning sixteen and becoming consumed with buying my own car to diminish my drive for all things motocross. My parents again made the same deal with me. If I could try to pay for half, then we could make it happen. This was a great lesson my parents instilled, showing me that you had to work hard to achieve your goals.

Football was everything where I grew up, and even more so for me than your average kid. My father, Alan, was a standout athlete at the University of Illinois who played with Dick Butkus and other legends. He often regaled my older brother Tate and me of flights to Pasadena to play in the Rose Bowl against USC. My dad had the chance to play in the NFL but chose to start a family and pursue a more typical career path. At that time, playing in the NFL was hardly the limelight and financial windfall it is today. My brother Tate was a star tight end at our high school and went on to a successful career playing for Furman University, winning several conference titles and a national championship in his freshman year in 1988. At 6 feet, 5 inches and 250 pounds, with good hands and a nasty side, he was just inches away from the NFL when he pulled a hamstring at the professional combine in front of prospective teams after his senior year. The chances of landing a spot on an NFL team are already razor thin and pulling your hamstring in front of a stadium full of scouts is not a good showing. His injury at that exact moment crushed his dream.

But the real star of our household was always my mother, Kathy. From first grade until I graduated from high school, she supported the three men in her life. She attended endless practices and games for both her sons, made sure there was more than enough food in the house for us and our friends, and was always there with unconditional love and support. It wasn't until later in my teenage years that she got a job, working as an interior designer. She just wanted to be there for us.

Just like the other men in my family, I was a football fanatic too. All the classic Southern high school football movie clichés applied to me. I drove a pickup truck, dated a darling little Southern belle cheerleader named Tara (see *Gone with the Wind*), and lived and breathed all things football. Strolling the high school hallways in my letter jacket adorned with patches, I felt like a king. My brother was a star at Wheeler High School, and I sought to continue the family's legacy. I was consumed with lifting weights, running countless sprints, and wanting to "hurt" running backs from rival high schools just down the road. As a linebacker, I idolized players like Brian Bosworth and Mike Singletary. The harder they hit, the happier I was.

My buddies and I were a tight-knit group of guys. Most of us were on the football team, and thus we were the celebrities in the hormonally driven halls of our school. During my junior year, we made a run toward the state championship game, no small feat in Georgia, where football is king. Our dreams of glory came to a screeching halt in the semifinals when we lost to a bigger and more talented team from down the road in Athens. We fought tooth and nail in the game and left everything we had on the field that night, losing by just one touchdown.

It seemed life could not get any better. Football players could get away with almost anything where I grew up. A lot of the clichés you hear about are true. I remember waiting in line for our high school graduation practice where we would receive our diploma, and out of nowhere, my guidance counselor frantically approached me. "Ryan, please tell me that you took English Literature 200 last semester; there seems to be something missing." Well, I had not, and already having signed a scholarship to play football in college, this was a somewhat worrisome situation. The counselor disappeared for some time and then found me again in line, casually mentioning, "Okay, you got a B in that class."

It's funny how sometimes it just takes that one pebble dislodging and rolling downhill to start a landslide. My life-altering decision to abandon the life I was blissfully following—football, college, wife, kids, beers in buddies' backyards—was still years in the future, but the first moments of that landslide started during my senior year in high school. That's when my friend Kevin and I watched a movie about American climbers dramatically scaling a mountain in Pakistan. The storyline would eventually become a real part of my life in the future. That movie was called *K2*, and it caused me to turn to Kevin in wide-eyed anticipation and say, "Let's learn how to rock climb!" That was my pebble.

Looking back now, it was crazy the way we got into rock climbing. Our experience was a far cry from the structured, safely managed classes and instruction found at today's climbing gyms. We would go out with light trekking boots, find some cliff of gneiss or granite along the Chattahoochee River basin, and start climbing as best we knew. We would often get ourselves into precarious positions high off the sloping, pine needle–covered ground below, but we always somehow got down safely. We toyed with the idea of investing in black fingerless gloves like Sylvester Stallone wore in the Hollywood blockbuster *Cliffhanger*, but we didn't. Thank goodness for that, since not one climber I have ever met has worn anything like that. Don't believe everything you see on the big screen.

I was hooked. Being on a rock face, slowly working my way skyward, was unlike anything I had ever done. The thrill of figuring out routes and extricating myself from sticky situations energized me. Little did my mother know where her innocent inquiry about what I wanted for my eighteenth birthday would lead. I wanted climbing gear, and she was about to inherit many sleepless nights worrying about her youngest son on the side of some mountain in Tibet or Pakistan.

We went to the local outdoor gear shop. The pretty blond girl behind the climbing counter introduced herself as Robyn. She patiently explained to my mother the essential equipment I would need to safely climb. She also casually mentioned that she had just returned from climbing for several months in France and was planning other adventures around the world with her boyfriend. My mother did not hear this last part; her attention was focused on the information about fall ratings of ropes, holding strength of harnesses, and how a certain webbing could support a small car.

On the other hand, I was mesmerized by Robyn and hearing how people could just travel around the world and do this kind of stuff for a living. How cool is that? That girl turned out to be Robyn Erbesfield, who would go on to become a world champion sport climber and eventually instruct some of the best junior rock climbers in America at my home climbing gym in Boulder, Colorado, some twenty years later. The climbing community can be a small world.

I left the store with a coil of BlueWater static climbing rope, a simple climbing harness, a figure 8 belay device, some carabiners, and tubular webbing to make anchors. I also left the store not knowing the first thing about how proper climbers actually used that gear. The concept of anchoring a rope and creating a belay system to safely climb to the top of a route I wanted to ascend by "toproping" was utterly foreign to me. Up until that moment, Kevin and I had just winged it when we were on the rock. But we were determined to keep pushing ourselves toward bigger and badder rocks, and we both knew that we would have to learn how to actually use the gear that I now owned. That summer, the two of us read everything we could find to teach ourselves how to actually climb correctly and hit the rock as much as possible before we both left for our respective colleges.

When I arrived at East Tennessee State University, I was wholly committed to be the best linebacker on the team. I was one of the stars on a high school team that had almost made it to the state championship game. I was good and knew it. My mental attitude screamed one thing: "The college game better look out, because here comes Ryan Waters."

I was brought back to earth pretty quickly. The speed of the game and the size of the players took a giant leap from high school to college. I realized that this was going to be hard. As a freshman, I knew there was no way I would actually play. I regularly practiced with the second team and even made the traveling squad when we went to our biggest game of the season against Division 1A Louisiana Tech. But as the season dragged on, I found myself continually rehabilitating a knee injury I had sustained in high school, and the job-like atmosphere surrounding college ball just wasn't resonating anymore with me.

My growing love affair with climbing came at the expense of football. Where once I could not imagine walking away from the sport that was so ingrained in my family's history, I now started to wonder if I might be done with it. If maybe the long, hot days of practice and the beating it was inflicting on my body were not worth it. I did not really enjoy that aspect much anymore.

It was a transformative time, one where I started to think about just being a typical student, not a student-athlete, something unthinkable just six months earlier. I believe that my growing love of the outdoors and climbing helped fuel those feelings. I agonized about what to do for several months, but in the end I chose to leave the football that I had loved for so long and transfer to Ole Miss to start a new chapter in my life. It was time to find out what interested me outside the insular world of sports.

As I would consistently learn over and over in my life, making big decisions to change your trajectory can have lasting positive effects on your life. I absolutely loved my time in Mississippi. Though my life had changed pretty dramatically from weight-training workouts, tackling drills, and running seemingly never-ending sprints to studying and a heavy dose of partying with my fraternity brothers, I really loved the new life I was creating. I was making lifelong friendships, and was able to breathe a bit and enjoy the experience of college. I wasn't necessarily a model student, but I was very committed to earning a degree in geology, my chosen path.

I still was kind of obsessed with rock climbing, but finding anything to climb in Mississippi is a tad challenging. The state is pretty damn flat. Any chance I got, I would talk a friend into driving over to northern Alabama to climb. We would head to some of the best rock climbing areas in the Southeast, like Horse Pens 40 or the Hospital Boulders, north of Birmingham. The climbing road trips at that point were not nearly as serious as they later would become. Especially since my crew of friends who had any interest in climbing also had a keener interest in partaking in recreational substances. There were many nights spent sitting around the campfire drinking and smoking, but what the hell? We were just emulating the life we read about in climbing magazines.

On the first day of my final physics class, one of those innocuous moments in time that alter your life's trajectory happened to me. Something that at the time seemed so simple but would create ripples that I still feel to this day.

During a particularly dull moment in the class (I think the professor was droning on about the Laws of Attraction), I found myself staring at the towering mountain on the cover of my textbook. It was a striking snow-covered peak that seemed to tower over everything else in the frame. I could not take my eyes off it. The inset description stated that the mountain was called Pumori, meaning "daughter mountain" in the Sherpa language. It was located near Mount Everest in Nepal. The caption also noted that it was thought by many to be the most beautiful mountain in the world. I agreed. I was mesmerized. Right then I made a naive promise that someday I would visit this mountain to climb its graceful slopes.

I left school armed with a degree in geology and not much of an idea of what to do next. I knew that I was ready to take the next step in life, but what that was escaped me. I did know that I was pretty worn out on the partying and such that surrounded fraternity life. Once I left school, I could see from an outside perspective that anyone can get drunk and throw a couch through a window, but these antics did not necessarily translate to becoming a responsible adult or make me truly happy.

Looking back with the wisdom that comes with age, I can see the first glimmers of understanding that I craved a life of adventure, one that was still a few years away from launching. When I applied for and got a job as a volunteer geologist at Arches National Park in Utah, I knew I should take it. The thought of driving west into the desert and beginning a real adventure like something out of the Edward Abbey novels I loved was very appealing. I was so close to taking it. But instead I chose to follow a more responsible path—though one I was to abandon in the not distant future. I moved to Atlanta and started doing environmental consulting with a geology firm. The pay was good, and in my mind this was the proper way to start an actual career, one that would lead to a stable life.

I liked what I was doing. It offered a nice mix of office and fieldwork. My work was respected, and my co-workers were good folks. Like most people in their early twenties, I was stumbling along, figuring things out one step at a time. But, regardless of the pay, praise, or prospects of promotion, I could slowly feel the restrictions that come with corporate life.

Throughout my time in Atlanta, I could feel the pull of the outdoors. It was always on my mind. I began reading every book I could get my hands on about expeditions around the world. Every weekend possible, I would head out of town with one of my college friends who also was into rock climbing, to climb in Tennessee or North Carolina. Gradually I discovered that I would rather go climbing all weekend than go out to bars and drink beer in the party district of Buckhead in Atlanta with the rest of my circle of friends. While I was in college at Ole Miss, I definitely had my share of fun (and have fond memories of that time), but I knew I wanted a change. I had this overwhelming feeling that life seemed a bit hopeless when you had to work all week long only to look forward to the weekend—one that was full of drinking Friday and Saturday nights and a hangover on Sunday. Then back for another week of work in a cubicle. It was a cycle I wanted to get out of.

This is about the time when the big mountains started to pique my interest as well. I was reading every mountaineering or Himalayan expedition book I could get my hands on. During this time, I first saw David Breshears and Ed Viesturs speak, two famous high-altitude climbers who would later become acquaintances of mine. I was becoming obsessed with climbing and expeditions. A one-page advertisement from the gear company Patagonia quickly became a makeshift origami envelope that I stashed my climbing trip money in. The image of people carrying kayaks across desolate landscapes on the way to climb a towering granite spire in the Patagonia region of Argentina inspired me.

I needed a change, and climbing was the way out for me. Looking back, I can see that I took steps to distance myself from normal, everyday life. Even though I did not need to financially, I took a part-time job at the gear store REI in the evenings and weekends to be around climbing gear and get deals on equipment. I really enjoyed the process of learning about different brands and talking with other like-minded individuals. REI was, and is, an island for those of us in society that are happier off dirty and dusty on the trails than socializing in bars and malls. Plus I learned more skills for climbing and was building out my ever-expanding array of climbing gear. My regular salary paid all my bills, and the money

I made at REI was spent in the store. I was living a double life, one that I think I knew even then was not sustainable.

My changing mindset was of no surprise to anyone who knew me. It was pretty much all that I talked about. It must have been apparent to anyone around me that a change needed to happen. When I walked into the manager's office at my job after three years of working there full time and announced that I was taking a job that upcoming summer as a climbing instructor for an outdoor education company in Asheville, North Carolina, they were not surprised.

On a whim, I had gone one weekend to an interview at Outward Bound's Cedar Rock Base Camp after randomly sending in an application and my rock climbing résumé. I guess the interview weekend went well, because a couple of weeks later, when I came home from the office, my roommate had propped up a letter from them on my door. It read, "We would like to hire you as an assistant instructor and climbing instructor at the North Carolina Outward Bound School." That was literally the moment I felt the direction of my life begin to take a significant turn.

I have developed a mantra over many years in the outdoor guiding industry: "You have to make things happen for yourself." I had suddenly slashed the safety cord of a solid salary, a 401k, and a comfortable career path that would have led to a wonderfully stable and likely more mundane life. Now I would be making $40 a day and living out of the back of my SUV at a base camp in the mountains of North Carolina, and I could not have been happier.

All the clothing and possessions I would need for an entire summer were stuffed into three duffle bags. A plastic locking storage container held all my climbing gear. Everything fit alongside a sleeping bag in the back of my vehicle. As I drove north, leaving the traffic-choked highways of Atlanta, I looked in my side-view mirror. I did not notice the other cars inching their way toward the city that morning. I was heading in the other direction. I only saw that my SUV was starting to get dusty, that my suburban life was fading.

Chapter Two

Margaritaville This Ain't

WHEN MY PARENTS FIRST TRAVELED TO VISIT ME IN THE HILLS NEAR Franklin, North Carolina, they were a bit taken aback by my bare-bones living situation. While they didn't know what to expect walking through the woods to my little cabin, they expected more than they encountered. The cabin was not much more than four plywood walls supporting a roof. Gone were the creature comforts they were used to seeing me surrounded by. I had traded a living room, kitchen, bathroom, and comfortable carpet for a wood-frame bed. Instead of art, the walls were covered in climbing gear hanging from hooks. They must have thought I had lost my mind. But I had carved out my own little refuge in a simple house with no electricity, a front porch often crowded with other instructors, and a bouldering wall a mere 10 feet away. Its simplicity and solitude were heavenly to me.

As we walked around the open, green grass fields that separated the Green Cove Base Camp structures, we met many other staff members who I introduced to my slightly dumbfounded parents. I was beaming when I showed them some of the nearby areas we used to teach students basic rock climbing. My excitement was evident to them, and I could slowly see my parents understanding why this place was special and why I had chosen this different pathway in my life. They were especially captivated by our resident program director, Pandora Judge—really, that was her name. Clad in Carhartt overalls, she was an athletic woman who had grown up farming in Vermont and was dating another young lady with purple hair who worked as a course director at our base camp. This must have been a totally eye-opening experience for my parents, coming from straight-laced Marietta, Georgia.

At that time, there was not even a shower at the base camp; we bathed in the nearby creek when needed. While sitting down for lunch with me in the modest buildings that we worked out of every day, surrounded by the somewhat smelly and smiling staff, I could see a glimmer of recognition in their eyes. They could see how happy I was. Not long after we ate, they were back on the road headed toward Atlanta. I don't know if it was the cast of characters surrounding me or the kale salad for lunch that my father eyed suspiciously, but they had had their fill. They definitely didn't quite understand what the hell I had gotten myself into, but they knew I was right where I needed to be.

I was working as an assistant climbing instructor under the watchful eyes of head climber Rob Dillon. The cozy hut that housed all the group gear—ropes, carabiners, and the like—was coated with climbing photographs of big walls from Yosemite to the Himalaya. It was a place for the climbing staff to lounge, have meetings, and pack gear before meeting groups at nearby crags to teach them rock climbing skills. Instead of driving, we would haul our gear in on our backs in full packs. We were tanned, taut, and in incredible shape, kind of like hippie versions of Hercules. At night we sat around drinking cheap beer, challenged each other to pull-up contests, and swapped stories about where we had been and what our next trips would be.

A legendary female alpinist named Kitty Calhoun had worked as a rock instructor at the base camp before me. She was rumored to have hiked up to five hours, each way, to the farthest crag while carrying a heavily laden backpack, renouncing the assistance of the vans at her disposal. She set the standard all strove to follow. It was almost like a competition to see who could suffer more, work longer days, and install new climbing routes on their days off.

I had basically decided that I wanted to be just like Scott Fischer, the legendary American guide and owner of Mountain Madness. He had died on Mount Everest in 1996. He, too, had come from a small town and discovered climbing. He had logged time learning the ropes as a climbing instructor at the National Outdoor Leadership School (NOLS), and stories had drifted around the industry about his work ethic. He would routinely carry one hundred pounds of gear while doing bicep curls with rocks he picked up along the trail. He said he "wanted to be the best climber in the world," so he was constantly pushing himself physically. It was a mentality that I embraced, and it permeated my lifestyle. I often look back on this formative time in my career and give thanks that I worked so hard. What I learned here has saved me from disaster more times than I can remember.

In life, you are constantly learning more about the things you think you already know, and I certainly had a lot to learn about instructing students on technical terrain. As a rock instructor, you do a lot of pretty straightforward classes on the ground. Hours pass teaching people the basics of how to tie knots and how to belay on simple rock walls, and motivating people to keep pushing for the top. One thing this does for you as a climber is instill solid "hard" (technical) skills that stay with you forever. The best way to learn something is to teach it.

On more significant routes, I learned how to effectively manage multiple climbers up multi-pitch routes. The first thing drilled into me is that longer routes are measured in rope lengths. After the climber in the lead covers roughly the length of a climbing rope, they must build an anchor with equipment placed in the rock features. The second climber can then make their way up to the anchor stance while on belay from above, and then the team climbs another rope length. Each of these rope lengths is called a pitch. Big climbs like the ones in Yosemite can require thirty-plus pitches to reach the top.

As an instructor, you seem to always find yourself in some new situation where you need to problem-solve. You have to learn how to motivate climbers on your rope to continue following you upward in potentially hazardous conditions. Priority one is to keep them safe, especially the less knowledgeable students, while gently reminding them of the goal of reaching the top. When they finally top out and their faces light up, all their worries from before seem to magically fade away. These are the "soft" skills that get embedded in your instructor's quiver of knowledge, and I rely on them even today while guiding people to the summit of Everest.

Getting good at something, anything, requires practice, more so when you want to become an instructor and a leader. If you wish to play guitar, shoot hoops, or climb rocks, you must spend days in that environment. The same holds true for getting into the outdoor industry. You may think you know a lot, but you don't. In general, guides and instructors land their first few jobs because they are strong at one of two things: Either their technical skills are solid, or their soft skills of working with people and good communication rock. Rarely does someone in their twenties possess both of these traits from the get-go. I had a decent amount of days logged climbing and trekking around the mountains of the United States. But I really didn't know the first thing about talking a teenager out of running away into the woods at night because they did not want to be there, or discussing the philosophy of life with a forty-five-year old surgeon who was taking a break from a hectic life to escape and learn about themselves. These are the things you slowly absorb from more experienced staff, picking up pieces of knowledge from the people you work with. Watching them react to a situation and seeing how they handle it is crucial. Slowly, over time, you develop your own style.

To work as an outdoor educator or guide and lead groups in the backcountry, you are required to take a wilderness first-aid course and get a Wilderness First Responder Certification. It was one of the most informative courses I had ever taken. Little did I know how much of that initial base level training would be put to use over the next two decades, from rescues on 8,000-meter mountains in the Himalayas to cold injuries on the Arctic Ocean. Being able to react and respond to emergencies as well as simple first-aid scenarios is also a skill progressively learned over time and with practice.

During my first summers bounding around the hills of North Carolina with teenagers, I saw lots of sprained ankles, bee stings, spider bites, and even a dislocated kneecap, which is pretty rare. These mishaps become pretty routine after treating them frequently, but the situations that were the scariest for me to manage were the objective hazards that were essentially out of my control.

Lightning is no stranger to the mountains of North Carolina, second only to Florida in strikes per year. Booming late afternoon storms would frequently sneak up from the other side of the mountain when we were 400 feet up. That's bad news when you are tied to two beginners that cannot quickly react or extract themselves from a precarious ledge. Or when paddling with students down a whitewater river far from shelter in a storm. One of the biggest motivators in perfecting my skills and having systems in place to handle emergencies came from dealing with situations like these. When the lightning was cracking in the sky overhead, I had to be able to react quickly and calmly, often while dealing with people paralyzed with fear. The technical skills and the soft skills needed to talk to and direct people in serious situations and act efficiently became second nature.

On one particular day, seemingly all my newfound skills were put to the test. I was on the third pitch up a granite dome we commonly used as the big culmination of our two-day rock course. Tied to me were two teenage girls who had, just the day before, learned to belay a fellow climber and use basic climbing techniques to ascend climbing routes. Technically, as an instructor, you were being belayed by the students as you led each of the rock pitches. But as beginners, these students had only practiced belaying a climber for a day or two. So as the lead climber, it was important to clip the rope into protection bolts drilled into the rock along the way until you reached the next anchor spot and built a belay stance.

Once there, you were ready to belay each climber coming up to you with the rope, which gave them safety. For instructors, the routes were not particularly challenging to climb. But your students were still figuring out the subtle skills of using a belay device, even if they had demonstrated proper belay technique. I always climbed with the mindset to never ever fall, just in case.

I had just arrived at the second to last belay anchor, over sixty feet above them, when the skies on the other side of the mountain almost instantly went menacing and dark. My students were tied into an anchor together on a small ledge below, connected to me by the thin climbing rope. I had to start making some decisions and quickly. It would take probably thirty minutes for each girl to climb to my location near the top of the route. However, we would still need to climb a short rock pitch, pack up the gear, and head back down. Plus, we would be in an exposed position for quite some time as we traversed a handline before we could start down the trail to get the hell off the lightning rod that we were on.

As I heard the first thunder rumble through the skies and the metal climbing gear clipped to my harness started buzzing, I paused to think for a moment. I made the calculations in my head and decided that getting down the mountain would be much faster by lowering them off the route. So I calmly shouted down to them, "Stay where you are clipped into the anchor; I will rappel back down to you guys." As I readied the second rope and rigged it to rappel back down, the sky cracked with lightning. I instantly gained concentration and weighed the severity of the situation that was unfolding. As I quickly rappelled the line toward the girls, I could hear them telling nervous jokes to each other, which is quite common when people get scared. As I reached their location and pulled my climbing rope back down to our belay stance, a lightning bolt ripped through the sky above our heads. These girls had fundamental rappel skills, so I took on the very straightforward instructor role of no longer teaching but guiding. "I am going to tie both of you guys into the same rope with a system known as a cow's tail. Don't worry, ya'll don't have to do anything, just walk backwards down the rock face together as I lower you to the next anchor. When you get there, I want you to clip in with the figure 8 on a bight knot we have practiced over and over, okay?"

Don't teach, just do. It's a motto many guides call on when things get sticky. As I lowered them about fifty vertical feet to the next anchor in the wall, we had a series of what we refer to as zero counts for lightning. That's when the amount of time between seeing a flash of lightning and hearing the boom of thunder is precisely zero seconds. Which means it is right on top of you. The girls began to scream, and my body felt electrified, no pun intended, as I reacted quickly to the situation. I again rappelled down to them. There was just one more pitch to go. I took a deep breath and re-rigged the system to lower them again as lightning struck the top of the mountain above us. We made it down, and I am sure those two girls have never forgotten that day. I sure haven't.

Not long before I started working at Cedar Rock, they had launched a program in southern Chile in the infamous Patagonia region, a mountain climbers' mecca. Only a few seasoned mountaineering instructors were trusted with running the small, clandestine operation in the challenging, windswept and often rain-soaked wildlands of the Lake District there. To work in the program, you had to be a jack of all trades—basically be able to do a little bit of everything. You had to help run the logistics, instruct, be able to guide on glaciers and to the summits of high-altitude mountains, and most importantly, be able to cope with living for months in remote small towns in Chile. Since I had always been fascinated by the images of far-flung granite towers in this wild part of the world, it became my near-term goal to somehow get a spot working there. Landing a position was challenging since the staff was very experienced and limited in size. Still, I was determined to do anything in my power to make it happen.

I guess I made a good impression in my first season as a rock instructor and assistant to the more senior staff in North Carolina. At the year-end staff dinner in Asheville, I was awarded the Thousand Mile Stare award. It was given to the climbing instructor that had worked like a dog all season and commonly would sit on a porch after work and just stare into the void. Hence the name of the award, which basically translated to logging tons of field days on the rock crags working with students. I was awarded a gift certificate for a free rock shoe resole, valuable currency for dirtbag climbing instructors.

During my three years working as a geologist and the off-season of that first year instructing rock climbing, I always yearned to learn the glacier skills needed to scale high-altitude mountains. My first experience with high-altitude climbing came when I signed up for a four-day mountaineering skills course on Mount Shasta, a 14,179-foot glaciated volcano in California. I loved the process of learning rope team travel, how to walk with crampons, and how to use an ice axe. Watching the two instructors on that trip taught me a lot about living in the alpine environment and the signs and symptoms of altitude illness, and I was infected by their passion for teaching on glaciers. Climbing in the night on a summit bid was exhilarating, and I felt so natural in that environment. Standing on the summit of my first 14er was like a religious experience for me. I was soon hooked on the world of big mountains as well as rock climbing!

During vacations, long weekends, and every chance I got, my climbing buddies and I challenged ourselves on progressively more difficult mountains in the western United States. We took road trips to the Cascade Mountains in Washington and Oregon and the Tetons in Wyoming to climb peaks like Mounts Rainier, Hood, Adams, and several in the Teton Range. We also took a weeklong trip to central Mexico to ascend 18,491-foot Pico de Orizaba and 17,159-foot Iztaccihuatl. It was my first time traveling internationally to climb, plus I could practice speaking Spanish.

So besides having had a good season working the crags of North Carolina granite, I also had amassed a pretty good base of personal mountaineering experience to fill in on my application to Patagonia. All they could do was tell me "no," so I went for it.

Against all odds, I landed a job for the next season in Patagonia. Somehow I had convinced them to let me work as the logistics person. As quick as I could grab a pen, I signed the contract without a second thought, committing myself to the entire season in Chile. This was perfect. The South American summer climbing season runs during our winter months, a time when I would not be working in North Carolina. I would be able to work year-round doing something that only a few years earlier would have seemed impossible. I arrived with my duffle bags packed to live for five months based 500 miles south of Santiago in the small leisure and adventure town of Pucon. I could not have been happier.

From the moment I arrived, I was in awe. The staff members working there were somewhat legendary figures among the community of Outward Bound instructors. They had created an entire program from scratch in the middle of a remote region of Latin America. Every single piece of gear had to be found and transported there, housing procured, curriculums created, plus a host of other issues resolved before the first twenty or so American clients could arrive. We were lodged in a four-bedroom house just a few blocks from downtown Pucon. It was basic but really nice inside, made with the carved rustic wood often seen in Patagonia. I was thrust into a living, breathing school of life where I had to learn on the go. The propane showers would scald you if you were not careful. The foods everyone ate were different from what I was used to. Changing my money into pesos was a chore. Everything was so exotic. Looking back now, after decades crisscrossing the globe, I can see how naive I was about the ways of the rest of the world that existed outside of the country I had grown up in.

It was a fantastic time for me. I was essentially a gopher, charged with packing the gear and food supplies. I worked with a local man named German; he always smiled and was super patient with me as I peppered him with questions. We would drive around town and out to rural locations to buy supplies and organize various aspects of upcoming trips. During my time with him, I learned how things really worked in Chile, something that would come in handy every single time I returned there to climb more peaks.

I was invited to join a staff training climb on a 12,293-foot volcano called Mount Lanin, which straddles the border of Chile and Argentina. We drove for several hours through the countryside and into the national park on gravel roads toward the *frontera*, a no-man's-land that separated the two countries. Large, snowcapped volcanoes began to appear on the horizon. At the end of the road, and I use the term "road" very loosely, we unloaded several days of supplies and began to hike toward a base camp just below a towering glacier. Watching the instructors seamlessly operate as a team was inspirational.

I distinctly remember lying in a tent that first night with a dynamic figure named Ted Alexander. Strong as an ox, with three-foot-long dreadlocks, he was born in England and raised in a literal cult-like-commune in Pennsylvania, which he had in his words "escaped." He had left his family's community with nothing and no plan to return. Somehow he ended up working as a climbing instructor for a few years and then migrated to Peru. On a lark, he decided to buy a rowboat and row the entire length of the Chilean coastline. It seemed only logical that he was one of the people tasked with creating the Patagonia Program for Outward Bound that I was now a part of.

In the next tent was Brady Robinson, the director of operations for the Patagonia Program. He had recently returned from an attempt to make the first ascent of K7 in Pakistan with Conrad Anker and Jimmy Chin. I was in a whole new league, and this was a far cry from my conservative Dixie upbringing. I was quickly discovering that not only was international travel an adventure, but the people and characters you met along the way were eye-opening and inspiring in their own right. That first night camped under the stars, I was in a trance, falling asleep with Ted's legs casually draped across my sleeping bag (which seemed quite weird to me) while he played Pink Floyd on his backpacking guitar under the Southern Cross in the sky above. I was blown away and knew for sure that this was the life I would live for the rest of my days.

I had a pretty good season in Chile working as the logistics guy, going on food shopping trips, arranging duffle bags for resupplies via horseback with gauchos, and generally cutting my teeth while living in international towns. I was still very wet behind the ears, but was soaking up everything I could from the more experienced mountaineers around me.

The "Four Pillars" that the Outward Bound program was built on—self-reliance, physical fitness, craftsmanship, and, above all, compassion—were beginning to strongly resonate with me. The courses were designed to deliver these ideas to the students, but at the same time, I also soaked these ideas up and saw firsthand how they made ordinary people quite extraordinary instructors. As I have gone on to become a mountain guide, these ideals are the way I live my life and are invaluable both in the wilderness and back home in the city. The lessons that the outdoors teaches you can and should be transferred to your everyday life. The whole idea of getting out of one's comfort zone and taking on a challenge is a life lesson. One that I embrace and encourage others to do, too.

Toward the end of the season, I went on a reconnaissance road trip to a little town east of our base camp in Chile. Brady, the program director, Dave Elmore, a veteran mountain instructor, and I took to the highway in the company truck. Our destination was Bariloche, a small adventure town on the other side of the towering Andes Mountains in Argentina, a country that would soon become one of my favorite places in the world. Perched on the southern hillside of one of the largest glacial lakes globally, Lago Nahuel Huapi, in the Lake District of northern Patagonia, the town was stunning and offered excellent access to some imposing peaks.

Unlike the Chilean side of the Andes, which is hit year-round with moisture coming in from the Pacific Ocean, the Argentina side is in the rain shadow, with a rugged, drier landscape and innumerable bluebird days. The overall vibe, or *onda* in Spanish, was markedly different. The Argentineans had a very European feel with an almost hippy mentality. They were beautiful people filled with a zest for life. I was instantly hooked.

It only took the three of us one night to start discussing what it would take to relocate the entire Patagonia operation to this side of the range in Argentina. The city and the area surrounding Bariloche were ideally suited for adventure and could open up a whole new set of courses. We could offer expeditions and classes on both sides of the Andes. Plus, we could expand operations in a new area by offering sea kayaking on the Pacific coast.

Before we could present our ideas to the higher-ups, we had to effectively scout the area. Well, that's what we told ourselves anyway. I think it was merely a perfect excuse to explore. We set out for a place above Bariloche called Tronador. It seemed the ideal spot for running mountaineering courses. We hired some gauchos to carry duffel bags of equipment to the two countries' frontier on the heavily glaciated slopes of 11,500-foot Cerro Tronador. It was a real adventure, one I had been dreaming of ever since arriving in South America. We literally had to figure out how to access and climb the more remote side of the mountain using local knowledge and topographic maps.

We made our camp for the night in the Paso Vuriloche, a mountain pass that humans had been using to cross the Andes since time immemorial. We pitched our tents at an unattended border checkpoint that was literally a log cabin in the forest and swapped stories around a crackling fire. The next morning, we woke early to make fresh-pressed coffee and prepared to navigate up the south ridgeline to access the alpine slopes above. Following only topographic maps and the advice from locals we had met in town, we picked our way up through a series of slopes covered in a mishmash of rock or snow. Eventually we reached an ancient stone hut perched on a high point of rock. Known as Refugio Viejo or "old hut," it offered little more than a roof and four walls in which one could escape the elements. I did not know then that this spot would hold many days of weathering storms, whiteouts, and even tragedies in the future, as I would follow this route many times while leading courses. We climbed the glaciers on the south side of the mountain and then traversed across the massive crevasse-laden cirque that separated the two international summits. As the sun began to bake us with reflections off the snow, it was time to traverse back north to the main *refugio*, which had a much easier trail system to descend back to a small outpost called Pampa Linda. It seemed like the perfect spot to run mountaineering courses. The funky vibe of Bariloche would inject a new life into the program going forward.

On a short break from work during the middle of that first season, I planned to join forces with an American female instructor named Laura Snider, travel up to Mendoza, Argentina, and climb the highest mountain in South America, Mount Aconcagua. At 22,841 feet, it is the tallest mountain in the Western Hemisphere and one of the Seven Summits, or the highest mountain on each of the seven continents. This would be my first really big peak, one that can be quite deadly, so we planned to follow the climbing guidebook down to the last detail. The two of us had a good rapport when climbing together, something crucial on big peaks. The wrong partner can ruin an expedition and be potentially dangerous. Laura was a solid rock climber, but this would be the first foray attempting a summit over 20,000 feet for both of us. We had plenty of technical skills. We had climbed high-altitude peaks in the United States and Mexico up to 18,800 feet tall. Still, Aconcagua, at 22,841 feet, felt like tackling a Himalayan peak.

It was the perfect challenge to take on at the time. The climbing route itself is mild, essentially high-altitude trekking. Still, it is a serious mountain with all the trappings that accompany high summit expeditions: bad weather, altitude considerations, and lots of strategy sessions. I loved the process of applying our skills to the planned two-week climb. We would ferry supplies up to progressively higher camps for the scheduled summit push, then head back down each night to acclimatize our bodies.

After spending about twelve days on the mountain, sleeping at Camps One and Two at successively higher elevations and then taking a short two-day rest at base camp, we were ready for a summit attempt. We made our way back up to Camp Berlin (Camp Three on the mountain) and slept there at 19,490 feet. It was a brutal night. Both of us felt terrible from the altitude, but we woke up anyway and brewed water in the dark to prepare to climb via headlamp. We set out for the top in somewhat marginal weather, unfortunately, because our time was almost up with regards to going back "home" to our jobs in Chile, and this would be our final chance to climb the mountain. After a few hours following the well-worn trail on loose rock, Laura started to get a terrible headache. We decided it would be better if she turned back for the high camp tent to recover while I kept climbing. She gave me a big hug, told me to be safe, and started back down the path we had struggled up.

I continued to climb upward alone. There were no other people on the upper mountain going for the summit that day. As the weather deteriorated around me, I pushed onward. We had pored endlessly over the guidebook in the days leading up to the climb, and I used my memory of the route to spot various features that told me I was on the correct path. I was focused on nabbing my first of the Seven Summits and thought nothing could stop me.

As I struggled upward in the infamously loose scree-covered slope, my energy started to ebb. By the time I reached the Canaleta, the last 300 vertical feet to the summit, I was exhausted. I was utterly alone, and the visibility had deteriorated to only fifteen feet in any direction due to a whiteout that had crept quietly over the mountain. An anxious internal voice started to say, "Don't continue; what if I cannot find the route back down?" All the signs came crashing down on me, pointing out that the prudent thing would be to turn around and get back to high camp before I got hopelessly lost forever on the highest of the Andean peaks. It would be a tough pill to swallow to turn around so close to reaching the summit. One I did not know if I *could* swallow.

But, as I knelt on one knee on the loose rock that stretched upward into the white cloud above me, I told myself for the first time in my young climbing career, "It is time to go down; the mountain will be here in the future." I knew it was the right thing to do. Reluctantly I turned my back to the tantalizingly close summit and began to descend into the mist. The decision quickly felt correct as I slowly followed the winding path down through stacked rock towers. The mist turned to a light snowfall, and the route slowly disappeared. Even if you have climbed a route many times, reversing the direction suddenly presents a mountaineer with a new and unfamiliar landscape. I became pretty worried as I followed what I thought was the correct pathway, while a bad headache settled in due to the lack of oxygen. But after a few hours I finally saw the rugged outline of the half-broken shelter at Camp Berlin. Laura was there, still battling her own headache. The pills she had begged off a nearby party of climbers had barely dulled it. The two of us fell into an uneasy sleep for the rest of the morning before packing up and carrying all the supplies back down to base camp in what felt like defeat.

After a day of licking our wounds and packing up our belongings for a mule to carry back to the trailhead, we started down from the base camp at Plaza de Mulas for a return to civilization. While trekking out from the mountain through the high, tan and red desert-banded hills, something dawned on me for the first time. I *could* make the difficult decision to turn around when things didn't feel right. This became the first precious lesson in my judgment on big mountain summit days that I would take with me for the rest of my career. The mountain would always be there, and I could always return.

After our failed attempt to reach the summit of Aconcagua, I had to report back to our base camp in Pucon, Chile, to begin work as an assistant instructor on my first program leading students on a fourteen-day mountaineering course. I learned a lot about navigating groups through rugged terrain that involved rudimentary and antiquated Chilean military topographic maps. Flanked by more senior staff that had come down from the Pacific Northwest school, I was able to take on my first leadership role in the Patagonia course area. It was terrific to be set free from the confines of the logistics department and actually work in the mountains! But the burning question of the Aconcagua climb was in the back of my head each and every night, and I found it hard to think about leaving South America without reaching that goal.

Before returning to the states, I stared longingly at my flexible return plane ticket. I just had to go back to finish what I started on Aconcagua. With a renewed sense of bravado, I made a plan to return again to Aconcagua with Dave, who had been on that initial recon of Bariloche in

Argentina. Collectively we were fit and fast, having worked a whole season, and totally in tune with the mountain environment. We packed light duffle bags at the Pucon base camp one evening, then caught a two-day series of overland buses to Mendoza. There was no time for fluff; we just wanted to get to the Aconcagua base camp and get the job done on the mountain. We basically raced up the mountain, reaching the summit just a few days after trekking into base camp. The whole trip from trailhead to summit and back to town took around seven days. It was exhilarating to knock off the climb, and I had a renewed sense of confidence.

During the expedition, Dave and I would sit around on the wind-battered rocks at 16,000 feet with a hot drink in hand and talk obsessively about the idea of someday establishing a mountain guiding company of our own. A couple of years later, we would formally start Mountain Professionals in Boulder, Colorado, conceived during what we like to call "the highest business meeting ever." It took us several years piecing together work for various organizations in different continents before we both deposited $500 into a joint business checking account and registered our business as Mountain Professionals LLC. Running an expedition company and traveling the globe to all the continents chasing adventures would soon become my primary career. All while guiding clients through successes, bitter learning experiences, and harrowing rescues of other teams.

After that first season working in South America, I decided to focus on my development as an instructor back in North Carolina for a year and try to get work year-round in the other programs offered by Outward Bound in new course areas. I wanted to take instructor training for both river and sea kayaking trips. I wanted to expand my abilities, plus they looked damn fun.

I also wanted to push my own limits and challenge myself to gain as much high-altitude experience as possible so I could rejoin the team in Patagonia and bring additional mountaineering acumen to the program. One of the other mottos I have developed over time is that "you have to take chances." I knew that there was no stopping this forward momentum building inside me from pursuing a mountaineering objective on a larger scale. Time was something I had plenty of, but financial freedom was in short supply. The only way to make money was to spend nights in tents working on courses, or get lucky and land a geology gig in the field to stash away funding. I was not sure what the next step was, but I knew that the towering peaks of Asia were drawing me to them. I took on every job I could to save money in case the right opportunity presented itself.

In 2002 I left the forest of our North Carolina base camp on an autumn afternoon, saying goodbye to the instructors with whom I had shared a summer full of joyful, carefree days. As dirt roads gave way to highways heading south, I looked at the passenger-side floorboard in my SUV/home. My college physics textbook stared back at me. That mountain on the cover, over 8,000 miles away on an entirely different continent, still called to me, louder now than ever. I promised myself that I would see it soon and stand atop it.

CHAPTER THREE

Time to Touch the Sky

I WAS IMMEDIATELY THRUST INTO A WORLD I HAD ONLY DREAMED OF the moment I stepped out of the red-brick terminal building at Tribhuvan International Airport in Kathmandu, Nepal. The whirlwind of smells, sights, and sounds threatened to overwhelm my senses. As I crawled into a battered taxi to head into town, my eyes were as wide as saucers. The place was so different, yet exactly how I pictured it from all the adventure novels and *National Geographics* I had read growing up. There were chattering street vendors hawking their wares, little kids chasing each other through dusty streets, and everywhere you looked, long, lean cows roaming free, often napping in the middle of the streets. I heard disco music, religious chants, and laughter all jumbled together. But best of all, off in the distance were the mountains, massive, glorious peaks shimmering through the ever-present layer of pollution that hangs over the city. They were distant beacons calling me.

It was the spring of 2003, and I had arrived in a much different Nepal than the one that exists today. Just two years prior, the king and essentially the entire royal family of Nepal had been murdered by the heir to the throne in a massacre. The country was now going through the middle of a political revolution led by a Maoist leader. Blackouts were a regular occurrence in the city due to power shortages, and there was no such thing as Wi-Fi then. I loved the raw humanity of the place.

I was there to join an international group of climbers for a four-week expedition into the heart of the Khumbu Valley to climb Pumori, just across the valley from Mount Everest. It was the peak I had obsessed over for years, ever since I saw it on the cover of my physics textbook. The anticipation of going on my first Himalayan expedition was intoxicating. I was armed with a lot of confidence, youth, and a burning desire to climb over 23,000 feet in the Himalayas, but honestly, not much else. I was almost shaking when I bought my plane ticket, I was so excited.

As everyone arrived, the next few days were magical, as any first experience somewhere new tends to be. I got to meet climbers from all over the world. We compared experiences and goals, and I was inspired by this crazy world of high-altitude mountain climbing from the start. I quickly felt myself slipping away from the rest of the world; I existed only here. Admittedly, that was much easier before the advent of Facebook and Instagram with their staged selfies and continual updates. Hell, I had even left my battered flip phone back home. My only connection to home was to visit an internet cafe using very slow dial-up internet to check my Hotmail account, or visit one of the many international phone call shops and sit in a booth. Instead, I roamed around with a camera and a few rolls of film. At night I would read a book by headlamp since rarely did the power stay on once the sun went down. I thought nothing could be better, until we flew deeper into Nepal.

As I stepped off the Twin Otter turboprop airplane to see prayer flags blowing in the wind at Lukla Airport, the historical launch point for Mount Everest expeditions, perched on a sloping ridge at an elevation of over 9,000 feet, my breath was taken away. The beauty of the mountains we had just flown into was overwhelming. I still get that feeling today when I fly in. From that moment the high, cold air of the Himalayan peaks and the Sherpa culture were instantly in my blood.

While trekking into the Khumbu Valley, I was humbled by the strength of the people in my team and, more importantly, the Sherpas who accompanied us. Interacting with these protectors of the peaks was so fulfilling. Drinking tea with them each day and hanging out with them in camp each night, learning about their culture and way of life, was a thrill.

The route to Pumori base camp is the same as the Everest Base Camp trek. This was the first of many treks up through historic villages such as Namche Bazaar and Tengboche. We visited the monasteries and shared the trail with the domesticated yaks used for ferrying loads and goods that stock the Sherpa tea houses along the way.

After reaching the base camp location, just beyond the last settlement of Gorak Shep, we said goodbye to our porters and their furry transports. They deposited all our food and climbing equipment to stage several weeks of climbing, turned around, and left. Only the climbing Sherpas stayed. I felt a real sense of pride when one day after we had been setting up camp, one of my expedition partners who had been in Nepal before told me, "You should be happy, the Sherpas are calling you Bai; it means 'little brother' and means they like you." My confidence was growing. I felt at home in Nepal, and to feel accepted by its people meant so much.

Part of guiding trips and partaking in expeditions across the planet is the chance to interact with many different peoples and their accompanying cultures. I have always tried to be an ambassador and treat everyone with respect while honoring their ways. It is so crucial in our ever-shrinking world. Some of my favorite people are the ones I have met out on the trail.

Over the next few days, we organized our gear and prepared. We laid out rotations for climbers to slowly work up and down the sides of the mountain in acclimatization trips, and began to settle into something I would soon come to know and love: base camp life.

Life in base camp is repetitive and straightforward but also inspiring. Each day you wake up to a Sherpa unzipping your tent door, asking in a kind voice, "Morning sir, hot tea or coffee?" You slowly unzip your sleeping bag to welcome the crisp, cold air until the sunlight finally hits your tent and begins to warm the new day. Stepping out into a valley of high peaks keeps you focused on why you are sleeping on the cold, hard ground for weeks on end. Rest days are spent relaxing, planning for the following days' rotations between the higher camps, and sorting gear. Time and the rest of the world outside seemingly stand still. You are in a place with other friends all working on a goal that has challenges and hardships baked into the very fabric of the objective. But once you embrace the climb and the passion of being on a big mountain climbing expedition, there is no other place in the world you would rather be.

On this expedition, I got my first experience fixing rope with the Sherpas on a big mountain. I offered to go with them any time they went high to push the route toward the next camp. Their strength and resolve to make progress on the climbing route was addictive.

It is not common for general climbing team members to get in and around the Sherpas' business when it comes to rope fixing, and even more so in current times. But back then, it seemed easier to grab the odd hunk of rope from a bag, carry extra gear, and somehow try to keep up with the boys long enough that they could see you were eager to help. The section between Camps One and Two was really the only part of the route where I had any chance to help out in small ways. Still, it was an incredible feeling to carry a spool of rope higher to a cache if needed. It felt like a dream come true.

Soon it was my time to head up on the last of our acclimatization trips before making a summit bid later on. After climbing for five hours, my partner, a German named Uli, and I reached Camp Two at an elevation of 20,341 feet, arriving on a narrow, rocky ridge that jutted dramatically from the east face of Pumori. The climb had not been especially difficult, but we were worn out from the early morning start and ready for a rest. We both sighed with pleasure as we took off our climbing harnesses, outer layers, and big mountaineering boots and crawled into one of the two tents that were anchored to a mixture of snow and rock on the side of the Himalayan peak. Below us, the Khumbu glacier we were sitting atop snaked downward, a frozen river of water, ever moving and shifting. The view was stunning, and I stopped for a moment and soaked it in. I could not imagine anything better.

It was a sunny day, and the inside of the tent was radiating the midday heat, so we took off more layers of clothing and laid inside our zipped-open sleeping bags in just our thermal underwear. As we melted water in the tent's front vestibule for a brew of midday coffee, I remember unzipping the back door for ventilation. I was admiring the route higher above us toward Camp Three. Our plan was to spend one night in the tents at Camp Three for acclimatization before descending the next day, part of a rotation all climbers must follow when partaking in high-altitude mountaineering, but I could not help thinking about going higher.

Above us the route meandered between snowfields, over or around dangerous crevasses, and up short, rocky steps. Dominating the entire landscape were massive hanging ice pinnacles clinging to overhanging parts of the glacier. Known as seracs, they are stunning to look at—huge slabs of blue ice perilously clinging to the sheet of snow and ice above— but also present one of the most dangerous elements of climbing. When these several-ton blocks break free, they trigger large avalanches that destroy everything in their path.

Suddenly, a loud crack sounded from the colossal hanging glacier above us, echoing down the slope. A large serac had given in to its fight with gravity. It crashed downward, burying itself into the pristine snowy slope. For a moment, nothing happened, and then a huge slab of snow came to life, cracks appearing everywhere as the snow slowly started sliding directly toward us. In an instant my mind processed the situation, and for the first time in my climbing career, I thought I might die.

As the avalanche hurtled toward us, there was nothing we could do to rectify the situation. I was going to die sitting in my sleeping bag with my boots off. All I could do was pull my bag around me, duck my head down, and pray. The roaring got louder by the second. I knew that soon it would be all over.

Where you place a camp on a mountain slope is extremely important and is a skill learned through years in the mountains. Our Camp Two had been established earlier by the Sherpas before we climbed. It was placed on the ridge jutting outward from the slopes above. So as the avalanche approached us, it violently slid down to the right and left of where we were precariously situated, like water finding the path of least resistance around a rock in a stream.

The mass of heavy ice and snow trailed away to either side, but the gentle, billowing ice particles rushing through the air found our tent as the main slide flew past our location. We were covered in a fine layer of dusted snow. We looked at each other and let out a boisterous laugh generated by nerves and relief. The adrenaline rush would take an hour to subside, and I don't think I slept a minute that night. I heard every single creak and moan emanating from the ice on the upper mountain.

Since that first real experience with a serious avalanche, I have been in and around many close calls on dozens of expeditions to far ranges, some situations much more intense and scary. Twelve years later, I would be in Everest Base Camp below that same Pumori mountain face when a massive serac of ice would be dislodged from essentially the same spot as this one and cause an avalanche that buried a large part of the camp, killing twenty-two.

Even though that moment was terrifying, it did not dampen my feelings of elation at being where I was. Ironically, while traveling to the Himalayas, I had been experiencing feelings of "burnout" from too many days in tents while working countless days on trips back home and in South America. I wondered if I was making the right choices in life. It only took a few weeks in the Himalayas to cure that feeling. I felt a renewed sense of rejuvenation as I learned additional techniques in such an elevated place. Plus, the mountains were incredible.

I am now familiar with the phenomenon that when you climb a higher-elevation mountain, climbing seems much more difficult in the cold and thin air. But as you progress in your ascension of higher peaks, you begin to develop an unexplained knowledge of your body and how it reacts. As you visit mountains over and over again, the hardships become blunted, and you become hard. You can't necessarily train yourself to be strong at altitude; it just seems to happen over time.

After a few rounds of climbing up to and back down from the camps for acclimatization, we were ready to make a summit push. When we reached Camp Three, located on the ridgeline straddling Nepal and Tibet, I was fascinated to peer into the arid, parched-looking landscape of the Tibetan side of the Himalayas for the first time.

Similar to Chile and Argentina, the Himalayas act as a buffer that creates a rain shadow effect. Moisture-laden air rises out of the Bay of Bengal in the south, where it hits a wall of mountains. As the soaked clouds struggle up and over these mighty peaks, most of their precipitation falls on Nepal, leaving the high Tibetan plateau fairly dry. The same thing happens in South America, where the saturated clouds rising off the Pacific Ocean deposit their rain and snow on Chile while struggling up the spine of that continent, leaving the eastern side in Argentina semi-arid. In fact, much of the movie *Seven Years in Tibet*, which chronicled the story of Heinrich Harrer and starred Brad Pitt, was actually filmed in Argentina because of the similar landscape (and cheaper cost of filming).

About two weeks after my experience with the avalanche, I found myself waking up to a freezing dark night at 21,325 feet. It was my first Himalayan summit day, something that warmed my heart at least. We climbed the winding path over the glaciers leading to the exposed east face of the summit pyramid as the sun began to crest the horizon. It was a magical feeling to be climbing my first Himalayan peak. Standing on the summit and looking across the valley to Mount Everest's mighty black pyramid, I felt inspired beyond words. I knew then that I wanted to experience this feeling again and again. I had successfully climbed my dream mountain, the one that had inspired me for so many years. And I would go back with more high-altitude experience and skills to help me as I pursued a job as a mountaineering instructor the following year in Patagonia.

On the trek out of base camp with my team and throughout the myriad beer drinking celebrations we partook in, that burnt-out mood I had been experiencing was long gone. I was already addicted to the heady feeling of being on an expedition in Nepal. It stuck with me as we hiked out and back past a progression of people in villages, then towns, and once again to Kathmandu. I made a decision on the trek out that I would fully commit to mountaineering and pursue any opportunity that presented itself, regardless of where on the planet it was. I only wanted to climb.

An opportunity presented itself shortly after that first Himalayan climb. For the 2004 Himalayan spring season, I was offered a position as an assistant leader on the northern Tibet side of Everest. But there was a caveat to the offer. I would not get paid for my service, and I would have to come up with $10,000 to secure my spot on the trip. Still, I jumped wholeheartedly at the opportunity to climb Everest. I now had an overriding goal that consumed my every thought from that moment forward.

Opportunity was presenting itself now because I was pushing my own limits and taking chances. I had a brand-new goal for the following spring: to climb the highest mountain in the world. But I had a lot of hurdles to overcome to actually make it happen.

Arriving back in the United States, I focused solely on instructing and saving money. I worked countless field days during the summer months for Outward Bound in North Carolina. One of the best ways to get lots of instructor days was to work as the proctor on a semester course. It meant a commitment of seventy-eight days in the field, which scared many people off, but not me. I landed a coveted position as proctor of the Appalachian to Andes Semester. It was perfect for me because I had the necessary skills and had no problem putting my life on hold for almost three months to work in three distinct locations with the same group of students.

The first twenty-six-day section was based in North Carolina and focused on general backpacking, rock climbing, and mountain living skills. The second section took us over to the Outer Banks of North Carolina for a comprehensive course on sea kayaks. We lived for days based out of waterproof dry sacks while traveling the fantastic coastline. All the while I was busy teaching expeditionary skills on water, such as reading tidal charts, planning crossings of open water, and how to survive on the ocean. From there, we did the final section in South America, focusing on mountaineering. It was an amazing experience.

I later became known as a glutton for punishment and proctored two more full-semester courses. I loved being in the field. To me, the long-form layout of semesters was much more rewarding to instruct because you got to know your students on a more fundamental level by spending so much time with them as a role model and teacher. I get messages from my students to this day, and it is so nice to relive those memories of the times we shared on adventures and see how their lives have progressed. Outward Bound still offers semester classes just like these. I recommend them to anyone looking for a change and a personal challenge.

I decided to stay in Patagonia once the semester was over to continue working on more mountaineering courses, live at the base camp for free, and sock away all the money I made. When I returned to Atlanta in February for the last few months before leaving for Nepal in April, I realized I was just a little short on funds for the expedition. So I reached out to my old geology company, the one I had worked for before diving full time into the outdoors. They were happy to sign me to a month-long contract doing geology work. I think they were a bit shocked at how much I had transformed in a few short years. It was strange to be making a hefty paycheck again while living in pristine hotel rooms and eating on a per diem each day. I saved every dollar I could, as I had a commitment to the Everest trip and was not about to risk the opportunity. I knew that this trip was the key to opening up future work for myself in the Himalayas, and my general climbing résumé would be developing in the direction I wanted it to. That reflected my evolving view of life, too.

Contrary to many mountain climbers who visualize reaching the top of a mountain as their ultimate goal when training, over the years I have developed a different mental vision. I focus on achieving the summit with so much energy left over that I could go over the mountain and down the other side. In other words, I try to look beyond the ultimate goal and focus on the next obstacle to tackle.

In reality, this is how everyone should train for high-altitude climbing because essentially, this is what you *have* to do. Except instead of going down the other side of the mountain, you must be able to reverse course and retrace your steps back to where you came from with plenty of stoke and energy left over to return to your high camp.

Also, contrary to common beliefs, living in low-elevation areas does not necessarily make it harder to go on high-altitude expeditions. I was living in Atlanta during the lead-up to my first 8,000-meter expedition on Mount Everest. Visualizing the success of standing on the summit was a piece of my daily routine, and I trained primarily by trekking up and down the very modest 1,808-foot mighty Mount Kennesaw. It is the highest point in the metro Atlanta area. Not exactly like the mountains I now have out my back door in Boulder, Colorado, but I made it work. Any trail that goes uphill is suitable for excellent mountaineering training. I would put music in my ears, load a backpack with rocks, and briskly trek up and down the chosen trail. If my knees started hurting, I would substitute the rocks for big water jugs that could be dumped out at the top of the hill (but then again, you can just drop the rocks out too).

I was also on the road a lot doing fieldwork for the geology firm, ironically in Florida at the time, an even flatter landscape. So I improvised. After eight hours standing behind a drill rig in the humid 100-degree heat, I would load up a backpack with phone books from my hotel room and hike the staircase over and over to the top floor and back down. Each time trying to beat my previous time. Many people think there is a secret recipe for getting in shape to climb big mountains, but honestly, the most valuable assets are grit and determination. My advice is to make an effort, months in advance, to push yourself on trails with heavy loads in a backpack while challenging your cardiovascular system going up and down hills. Essentially, you need to bust your ass.

When I landed in Kathmandu that spring of 2004, it felt familiar, and I loved being back. We had a large team made up of some twenty climbers from the United States, England, and several European countries. We would be climbing Mount Everest from the northern Tibet side of the mountain instead of the traditional Nepal side that most expeditions embark from. I was working as an assistant leader of the expedition. Although my Himalayan experience was not extensive, I was a mountaineering instructor. I had the experience of climbing over 23,000 feet on Pumori. I provided leadership as an assistant but did not have to worry about the overall expedition management. This was nice because right away we had issues due to the political instability in Nepal at the time.

The mid-1990s were a tumultuous time in Nepal. The Communist Party of Nepal, known as Maoists, began to claim leadership in parts of the country. They were in direct opposition to the kingdom structure ruled by a monarchy that had been in place for over 230 years, since the country was founded. Civil war broke out. It was a battle for the hearts and minds of rural Nepali people. It seemed that no one really knew who to turn to for leadership for many years, and things were complicated. As the support for the royal family began to wane, more and more Nepalis wanted a more democratic style of government structure.

Things got really crazy when on June 1, 2001, the heir to the throne, Dipendra Bir Bikram Shah, essentially committed what is referred to as the "royal massacre" in the palace in downtown Kathmandu. The story is shrouded in conspiracy theories and intriguing drama, and seemingly every Sherpa I have asked has a different opinion about what really happened. Essentially, the crown prince of Nepal killed most of his own royal family, including his father the king, before apparently committing suicide on that fateful evening in the royal palace. Nepal was in turmoil. Dipendra's uncle, basically the only family member who just happened to be away during the massacre, became the king of Nepal, thus fueling many conspiracies.

The Maoist party did not recognize the monarchy as the ruling government, which created havoc in Nepal's rural country, creating blockades, shutdowns of essential services, and the like. The chaos surrounding this power struggle continued until the monarchy was abolished in 2008.

Our Everest expedition was planning to drive across the Friendship Bridge on the border of Nepal and Tibet (China). That unraveled quickly upon arrival. A hastily announced blockade to all road traffic meant we had to get creative. That meant hiring antiquated Russian Mi-17 helicopters to ferry us over the roadblocks to the border town of Tatopani, creating a massive headache and expense.

I have two profound memories of that helicopter trip. The first was arriving at the runway to see our overweight Russian pilot, his gut stretching his flight suit taut, bent over an open engine muttering under his breath. This was while he was banging on the engine with a ball-peen hammer as the crew loaded thousands of pounds of our gear in through the back cargo door. It was not a scene to inspire confidence. The second occurred somewhere during the flight. We landed in a random open field along the way. Our pilot jumped out of the helicopter with the engine still running and ran into a nearby stand of trees. He was gone for about ten minutes—all of us wondering what the hell was going on—then he returned, strapped in, and flew us the rest of the way to the border. I would later hear that he had apparently paid off the Maoist hired guns hiding in the hills to not shoot at our helicopter as we disregarded their travel blockade.

Eventually, we made it across the land border into Tibet and started the long, bumpy, and dusty overland drive to base camp via four-wheel-drive Land Cruisers. The expedition was underway, with all the magic you would expect from your first trip to climb Mount Everest. Tibet is a fascinating place—arid, ancient feeling, and vast. At villages along the way, I would sit with the locals, take photos, and simply ponder in amazement how far I had come in my dream to go on expeditions. Three years before, I had been cooped up in a cubicle inputting data into spreadsheets while dreaming of a place like Tibet, and now here I was. A feeling of immense gratitude at my decision to take a chance permeated the entire trip. I had taken a leap of faith and landed in the exact place I wanted to be.

There were way fewer climbers in those days on the Tibet side of Everest as opposed to today. But even then, the gravel road went all the way to Everest Base Camp, which nowadays seems to welcome ever-increasing crowds of tourist groups, mostly from mainland China cities. The legendary Rongbuk Monastery, dating back to 1902, sits adjacent and just north of the base camp location at over 16,400 feet in elevation.

We moved into camp with nervous anticipation, took pictures at the Puja ceremony, sized up other teams' base camp setups, and mostly worried about our own personal preparations and whether we had what it took to get to the top.

The Puja ceremony is something I had experienced once before during the trip to Pumori in Nepal, but an Everest-sized one with a large team is a more dramatic event. It takes about three hours, more or less, and is restricted to specific days deemed promising by the monks and Sherpas, which are decided on a few days before the actual ceremony takes place.

It is an essential part of a climbing trip to the Himalayan mountains. A lama or respected Buddhist monk is asked to read a prayer at a stone chorten built by the Sherpas in base camp. The prayer is meant to request blessings or to invoke help in safe passage during a journey. Commonly accompanied by the rainbow of prayer flags synonymous with the region, and often wrapped up with copious amounts of alcoholic libations to close the ceremony, a Puja can be almost surreal.

The Tibet-side Everest Base Camp is unique in its relatively close location to an actual road. I will never forget the strange feeling of relaxing in my personal tent with the doors zipped open for ventilation or taking a bath of hot water from bowls while lounging on rocks, only to have a Chinese tourist fresh off the bus from Beijing walk up and take my picture out of curiosity about Everest climbers. You almost felt like a novelty, some strange zoo attraction.

The Tibetan people are extremely warm and welcoming to visitors. However, the mountain operations themselves are mainly run by Chinese officials who tend to be a bit sterner and more bureaucratic. It was fascinating for me to watch the yak drivers wander about the landscape. They wore mainly traditional clothing and spent most of their lives wandering in the most picturesque landscape you can imagine. Most practiced the Buddhist religion and were gentle people looking to earn a living from their trusty yaks.

I remember lying with my head outside the tent one day observing these guys walk around base camp. When they came across the odd item of old gear or discarded piece of expedition cookware among the rocks, they would pick it up and stare at it for a moment, taking in the object to figure out what it was, turning it over and over. In my mind, I could hear their thoughts clear as day: "Is this something that is useful to me in any way?" If the answer was no, they would just drop it back on the ground and keep walking. For some reason, that human-animal essential resourceful trait has always stuck in my mind.

I also saw the darker side of that human animal when I witnessed my first knife fight. Two yak drivers began arguing over something, and the conflict escalated. They yelled louder and louder at each other, gathering a crowd of onlookers. Just when the locals started to move in to break up the fight, one of the two men pulled out a knife. Then the second one did too, and they danced around each other, yelling and threatening. I could not understand their words, but the message was quite clear. They were ready to draw blood. Finally, the surrounding mob broke them up before anything tragic happened. They may have been gentle Buddhists, but they could lose their tempers too.

Over the next few weeks, we worked through our rotations up and down the mountain as we acclimatized and prepared for the inevitable day when we would make the final push to the top. Several climbers had to drop out when their bodies failed them during this period. I had quite a scare one day when I returned to advanced base camp (ABC) after rushing on a nearly fourteen-mile trek with an elevation gain of 3,937 feet. I lay in my tent and progressively felt worse as evening approached. By the time dinner was announced, I felt like absolute hell. I had developed acute mountain sickness (AMS) and had one of the worst nights in my life. Luckily my tent mate was a doctor and loaded me up with Diamox and dexamethasone pills to combat the onset of worsening symptoms. The following day I turned tail and slowly walked back to base camp. I needed to rest for several days at the lower elevation of base camp to repair my body. It was a real wake-up call. No matter how strong you think you are, it is paramount that you take the time to slowly acclimate and not push too hard between camps.

After the rest, I returned to a feeling of strength and confidence. I was thirty years old and brimming with enthusiasm. I reveled in the base camp atmosphere in between climbing days, getting to know my fellow climbers and Sherpas better over hot cups of tea and hot meals inside our dining tents at base camp and advanced base camp high above.

After making several rotations to Camps One and Two to acclimatize, we headed to the village of Tingri for an extended rest of several days at 14,108 feet. Tingri is not the most spectacular little town in the world. In fact, we said it was the place where dreams are made and then broken. I hear it is much nicer these days, but man, was it a dump back then. Nevertheless, it was a good place to recharge the body; when it came time to leave, I felt good. We caught a ride in a four-wheel drive back to base camp, and then suddenly it was time for my rotation to head toward the top to Camp Four for my attempt at the summit. I was to be part of the second group of climbers in a series of three different groupings. We spaced them out over several days of projected good weather.

This allowed one large team to rotate through the same tents and supplies at the higher camps, thus saving resources.

Our group packed up ever so carefully and set out for ABC once again to sleep a few nights before working up through the progressively higher camps. We reached Camp Four at 27,230 feet the day before our planned summit day.

The route to the summit on the Tibetan side is challenging due to its sustained climbing at high elevation along the Northeast Ridge. There are three significant hurdles, known as the First, Second, and Third Steps, each a distinct rock feature you must climb over along the way. As I labored over the First Step at 27,887 feet in the dark, working along the fixed ropes up and over a series of never-ending ledges of rock, I remember thinking this was quite challenging, something I had never dealt with this high up. The wind and bitter cold ripped at my down suit, and only the thin beams of light coming off other climbers' headlamps illuminated the way.

But once you get past that feature, you finally gain the main ridge proper, and in my mind the climbing was much more straightforward. Along that ridge is where you see your first dead bodies on the Everest route. You encounter a morbid landmark when you are forced to step over the legs of "Green Boots," a climber thought to be Indian Tsewang Paljor, who was wearing green Koflach mountaineering boots when he died. His body is curled up in a small alcove of rock along the trail. He is thought to have perished in the 1996 storm made infamous in Jon Krakauer's book *Into Thin Air*.

Somewhere along the ridge, the sun began to crest the horizon, and I could make out features along the rise ahead. We continued to climb along the ridge until reaching the ominous-looking wall of rock located at 28,248 feet known as the Second Step, which guards the final stretch to the summit of Everest. It is about one hundred feet of vertical rock that gets increasingly steep as you near the top. Thankfully the ladder anchored to the wall by a prior expedition made it reasonably straightforward to ascend, just really tiring, of course, due to the extreme altitude.

Once we topped out above the Second Step, I was confident that we would make the summit. The weather was perfect: blue skies and low

wind. The Third Step, the final technical rocky section, though still difficult, seemed to go by with less physical strength, most likely because by
then I was focused on the summit.

Traversing the north side of the final summit rise of Everest was an
otherworldly experience. The sun was up and cast a pyramidal shadow
on the landscape stretching to the west. I remember finally seeing figures
standing on a high point in red down suits and thanking the spirits above
that the summit was finally in view. For Everest climbers, the final steps
to the top seem to last an eternity, but your determination takes over, and
you will yourself to keep climbing. When our team reached the summit,
I felt a wave of emotions, including relief that there was no more damn
uphill!

I felt happiness, elation, and a sense of pride, and I let out a scream
of joy inside my oxygen mask. I had climbed my first 8,000-meter
peak—the summit of Mount Everest, the highest mountain on earth.
I felt fortunate to have been able to summit on my first attempt. Many
more accomplished alpinists were not as lucky with weather or route
conditions or any number of factors throughout the years. So with a
healthy dose of respect and admiration for the mountain, we turned and
descended, thankful that Chomolungma, the Buddhist name for Mount
Everest, which means "Goddess Mother of the Earth," had allowed us to
stand on her summit.

When we got back to base camp, my feeling of pride grew. Not only
had I reached the summit on my first try, but I had also helped several
other climbers make it there too. I had contributed in my leadership
position, and I started to realize that with a little more seasoning, I too
could organize and lead expeditions into remote and wild places. My
dream was beginning to become more real every day. I had chosen the
correct pathway in my life. Not everyone might understand it, especially
my parents, but I knew in my heart that this was where I needed to be.

Upon reaching Kathmandu, and with a week of extra time to spare, I
checked myself into the Kathmandu Guest House in downtown Thamel
and let the partying begin. Several members of our team stayed there,
and we basically enjoyed ourselves as you do after a Himalayan summit.

In the next-door room for several days was Jean-Christophe Lafaille, the famous French mountaineer who was arguably one of the world's best alpinists. He and his beautiful wife Katia and their children would share a coffee with me on the outdoor patio in the morning as I tried to soak up any wisdom from him through muddled mixes of French and English. He was someone I did not get to know well but instantly knew was remarkable, and I felt a great appreciation to even meet him. He would die in 2006 while attempting the first winter ascent of Makalu, which would have been his twelfth 8,000-meter summit, all of which he did by new routes and without supplemental oxygen. To put it simply, he was hardcore.

Later in my career, I would learn that sometimes the people you cross paths with, or, in some cases, even make plans to climb with, you do not see again. It is an unfortunate part of the big mountain game.

I now had a lot of mental momentum to carry forward—two Himalayan expeditions and two summits. When asked if I would like to take a step up and act as the leader of an expedition the following autumn to 26,906-foot Cho Oyu, the sixth-highest mountain in the world, I again jumped at the chance. It would be the first time that I would have all the responsibilities of an expedition on a Himalayan 8,000-meter mountain. Everything from pre-trip meetings, to logistics in Tibet, to guiding to the summit would be squarely on my shoulders.

Looking back, I consider this the start of a magical few years. During this time, I balanced guiding work and a little bit of geology consulting work, and mostly traveled part of the world on a rotation between the United States, South America, and Asia. I was unattached to any relationship, mortgage payments, or real commitments, so I made the most of that time.

During the expedition in the autumn of 2004 on Cho Oyu, I felt pretty strong. I even guided the summit day without personally using supplemental oxygen. Four-liter oxygen tanks are commonly used in the commercial guiding of 8,000-meter mountains in the Himalayas because they provide added warmth, oxygen, and strength for climbers, but I felt strong enough to climb without the assistance. The expedition was a success, with many client summits. We even had the first Sherpa female summit Cho Oyu on our expedition that year. This was a confidence builder from the standpoint of opening up higher elevations I could guide and the experience I was gaining.

It also got me the offer to lead an expedition to Everest from the Tibet side in the spring of 2005 and then lead a Cho Oyu expedition in autumn that same year. My Everest trip in 2003 had been successful, and I learned a great deal about being in charge of the myriad logistics, payments, client care, and managing staff that it takes to lead an Everest expedition.

On the previous Everest trip, I had felt in top shape the entire time, and I was eager to try to bag my second summit of Everest in as many years, but on our summit push in late May, by the time we reached our Camp Two on the North Col, I had caught a chest infection out of nowhere. Simply lousy timing. I chose to sit out the summit day so that I would not slow down the team. Instead, I stayed on the North Col as support and handed off the summit team to our Sherpa staff to lead.

In hindsight, though it was a hard decision to make at the time, it did prove that I was developing additional wherewithal on how to manage situations when it came to the health of climbers. It was a tough pill to swallow, but I don't regret not trying for the summit that year.

When I led another successful expedition up Cho Oyu that autumn, I felt ready to take the next steps in my career. In two and a half years, I had climbed three 8,000-meter peaks. I had worked my way up the ladder in expedition management and knew that it was something I liked and was good at. Leading clients to their dreams was fulfilling, plus it let me chase my dreams too. As I headed back to the United States that fall, I decided to reach out to my friend Dave Elmore to see if he might want to start a guide service with me. We had discussed it in depth on Aconcagua, but I wondered if he was still interested. I called him, and he leaped at the idea. He was at a similar phase in his life and had been thinking about putting down some roots, or at least having his gear located in one place.

As 2005 wound down, the two of us pulled the trigger and launched Mountain Professionals. Both of us were vagabond journeymen outdoor instructors with unstable living situations and rotating storage units, not exactly the best candidates to start a business. But what we did have was knowledge, passion for the idea, and the drive to put things in place.

In Boulder, Colorado, that winter, while sleeping on a friend and co-instructor's townhouse floor, we drove to the bank. Each of us deposited a $500 check into a business account and then appropriately headed to the local brewpub for our first official business meeting and drinks on the company credit card. We were off to the races at a snail's pace. We had zero official clients, no insurance coverage yet, and no gear besides our own personal equipment. It was one of the most exciting times I can remember.

CHAPTER FOUR

The Luckiest Unlucky Guy in the World

ONE OF THE INTERESTING ASPECTS OF ADULT LIFE IS TO LOOK BACK AT your past and imagine how you actually got by on having almost no money. One of the greatest parts of the life I had chosen—to chase adventures, travel, and climb mountains—was that I had lots of freedom. It did not take much income to feel perfectly content. I was able to say yes to all kinds of work worldwide while also pursuing my own objectives in the mountains. All I had to do was work a ton of days to finance a trip, but it didn't matter because work was fun too!

As you grow older, you acquire more things and life gets more complicated. Things cost money and take up space. When your business grows, your expenses increase and you have more responsibility. And then there are the relationships you eagerly pursue, only to find that sometimes they hinder your freedom to disappear and climb unencumbered.

I didn't have a solid plan for making a real income, but it didn't matter to me then. All I knew was that I loved being out on expeditions, and if I could make a daily wage doing it, all the better.

I had already been to the Himalayas to lead or work on two Everest expeditions and a Cho Oyu trip. I had also firmly solidified my coveted position as an instructor in the Patagonia Program, which would offer plenty of work through the October to February time frame of any given year. So I thought I should apply to one of the larger American guiding companies for the summer. That way, I could gain additional skills with clients by guiding laps up and down one of the mountains in the Cascade Range.

I was determined to create the perfect yearly work scenario: summer in the United States guiding, winter in South America instructing mountaineering, and autumn and spring free for exploring my burgeoning passion in the Himalayas.

I applied to and was hired by Rainier Mountaineering Inc. (RMI) in Ashford, Washington, whose headquarters was located at the base of one of the classic and historical American alpine mountains, 14,410-foot Mount Rainier. The owners and many of the staff were basically legends in the American mountaineering world, starting with the Whittaker twin brothers, Jim and Lou. They had started the company in 1969. Jim had become the first American to reach the summit of Mount Everest, and Lou was a veteran of many Himalayan expeditions. Lou's son Peter now ran the company. Many of the senior guides had big names like Ed Viesturs and Dave Hahn. The regular experienced guide staff list was familiar to me, as I had in the past pored over the names of guides working in the industry, including luminaries such as Brent Okita, Casey Grom, Jeff Justman, Mark Tucker, and Garrett Madison. In my incoming guide class alone were Melissa Arnot (the first American woman to climb Everest without oxygen), Seth Waterfall, Chad Peele, and many other accomplished and well-known guides who went on to have successful careers.

I took a lot of additional training at RMI that summer. I learned an immense amount doing laps on Rainier all summer long, developing solid guiding skills by learning from yet another host of more experienced guides in a different setting. It was great for getting in shape, too. Having already climbed Mount Everest lent me a cachet with clients and management, since that always looks good on a résumé. At the end of the summer, I was asked to give a speech at the Rainier Mountain Festival. I found myself on a stage with Lou Whittaker, Ed Viesturs, Pete Schoening, and other luminaries that I had read about in numerous books and magazine articles just a few years before.

After working on lots of trips with eager clients on Rainier, I made many contacts for future mountain climbs. It was very valuable for me to bring in names of potential clients for the future of our company,

Mountain Professionals, which was slowly beginning to gain a small amount of momentum. Luckily, it was not a conflict of interest at that time because RMI still had not committed to running a true international program. Specifically, the Seven Summits were not on their offer sheet yet.

Dave and I decided that we had to start pursuing clients for trips to the Seven Summits, the highest mountain on each continent. This challenge had morphed into a whole industry by this time. The commercial guiding of these mountains had become the primary revenue stream for several American and European guide services for years.

In the early 2000s websites for companies were laughably drab compared to today's standards. Dave and I had built an elementary site to display the trips we hoped to fill with clients. I focused on making logistics contacts with locals in Tanzania, Russia, and elsewhere. It is crucial to have a good partner in the various destinations to handle the on-ground logistics, store your company's equipment, and oversee the hiring of local staff.

We managed to piece together our first trips to mountains like Aconcagua and Kilimanjaro through word of mouth and past clients of our own previous adventures. Our world of guiding the Seven Summits was taking shape at a snail's pace. But for me, I suddenly found myself having climbed three of these peaks simply through work: Everest, Aconcagua, and Kilimanjaro. Back when I was a twenty-year-old, reading Dick Bass's classic novel *Seven Summits*, the possibility of climbing these mountains seemed out of reach. It is expensive and difficult to reach places like Antarctica and Indonesia, or even Everest for that matter, so the thought of doing the Seven Summits had always been a far-off idea. But now it was becoming a real option for me to tick off the rest of those peaks by guiding them. I made an internal and essential personal goal to finish climbing all the Seven Summits as soon as I could make it happen. I wanted to do it for myself, but I also recognized that it was an essential résumé piece for me and our company.

In the fall of 2006, I got the chance to lead another trip to Cho Oyu in Tibet. We had a successful journey, with all the clients reaching the summit, and I managed to climb that summit for the second time without supplemental oxygen. Mountain climbers have short memories when it comes to the hardships faced on a day-to-day basis while on big expeditions. It is common for people—professional climbers and clients alike—to dread the uncomfortable moments, like freezing mornings with frost on the tent and digging out snowdrifts. Sleepless nights in wind-battered tents evoke thoughts of "why am I doing this?" But after a week of life in the everyday world, we find ourselves hopelessly researching the next big challenge.

The irony of taking part in so many 8,000-meter expeditions is that over the years, I mostly remember the people and experiences tied to various trips, more so than the countless days spent on the mountains. The post-summit celebration day back in the small village of Tingri, Tibet, on the 2006 Cho Oyu trip stands out as one of the few single experiences I can really remember without looking back at old photos to jog my memory.

That night, arm in arm with clients, staff, and a group of five Chinese uniformed soldiers, I remember the dimly lit karaoke bar with cheap neon lights blinking in the window of a ramshackle wooden building. We belted out the lyrics to Madonna's "Like a Virgin" among a pyramid of empty Budweiser cans. The next morning, hungover and waiting to catch our four-wheel-drive Land Cruiser to the Nepal border, I distinctly remember seeking out one of the two slots in the roof of the "toilet facility." It was open-aired and had clear views of Mount Everest across the plains. So I was perplexed when one of my teammates decided to go ahead and squat next to me directly on the adjoining hole. I just needed some quiet peace for a moment.

When one of the Chinese soldiers from the previous night saddled up to urinate on the final remaining hole, my peace was shattered. Then something hysterical happened. Just as my friend was finishing his business and tossing his paper into the hole, a strong wind blew up. It sent the small square of soiled paper fluttering in the air for a few moments, only to land squarely on the boot of the soldier, used side down. A one in a million shot. Obviously annoyed yet surprisingly calm, he simply shook his foot in the air to free the suspect paper, yelled something in his native language, zipped up his trousers and lit a cigarette, and walked off. We looked at each other and silently chuckled. It was time to get out of Tibet and back to Nepal. Funny what you remember from specific expeditions after twenty years of adventures in the Himalayas.

With five Himalayan expeditions under my belt, it was time to return to South America for the winter. I loved being in South America when I was not on one of my more extended international expeditions. Just living in a town far away from home made each and every day feel like an adventure. That 2006 year was the real beginning of a lengthy career of instructing mountain courses on what would add up to more than 300 field days over many years in the Patagonia area alone. I was in love with Argentina and decided that I might as well just rent an apartment in Bariloche and live there instead of in the United States between my travels to other work locations such as Nepal, Tanzania, or Tibet.

Bariloche is both rugged and beautiful, remote and close. It is located far down in the middle of Argentina, close to the Chile border, yet it's merely a couple-hour flight from Buenos Aires. There are numerous areas to climb, bike, paddle, and get lost in northern Patagonia. Yet there are pubs and clubs and swanky hotels, as it's one of the places where well-heeled Argentinians and Brazilians go to escape for ski trips and adventures.

I also began to notice the women of Argentina more and more. Spending enough time in Bariloche, I became sort of a semi-transient resident and not just some lowly gringo tourist that was passing through on a three-day holiday to take Spanish classes. Moreover, since I had an actual apartment, it became much easier to convince a local girl that I might stick around a little while. Thus it lent instant credibility when I feebly approached the often-standoffish Argentinian women. These were my first experiences dating girls from another country besides my own, and it was an exciting time, to say the least.

One day in between some mountaineering courses, I got a call from one of my good friends and co-workers in Bariloche named Diego Magaldi. He wanted to know if I would like to give a talk and slideshow on climbing in the Himalayas during one of the evening breaks on a Wilderness First Responder course he was instructing. I figured it would be entertaining to try to give a speech for the first time, all in Spanish, to a group of budding Argentinian outdoor professionals or people interested in the outdoors enough to take a weeklong first-aid course. The forested collective of houses on the outskirts of Bariloche named Colonia Suiza was my destination on the bus. I gazed out the windows looking at the sights as we weaved over dusty dirt roads to a cabin where I had spent many days with students of my own. I didn't sense the happy upheaval in my life just on the horizon.

I always enjoy giving speeches about amazing trips I have been on. So it was easy to have confidence going into the room. Still, as I stumbled through each photo of Nepal, there was some laughter from the crowd at my mispronounced words, but I didn't let it rattle me. Then, about halfway through, a woman in the class caught my eye. I was struck by her natural beauty but kept going with my speech, which detailed my climbing experiences up to that point in Nepal, including Everest.

After consistently stumbling over the word for "oxygen" in Spanish multiple times, I finally wrapped up the talk to mostly energetic cheers. I thanked the group for having me, then escaped downstairs to the kitchen area to grab a beer. To my surprise, into the room comes the girl, seemingly going out of her way just a little bit to run into me. I introduced myself, and she did as well in an Argentinian Castellano accent. "My name is Alexia," she said.

My heart instantly skipped a beat. We chatted briefly. She told me she was taking the class because she had an interest in becoming a trekking guide. I, of course, explained to her that I was living in Bariloche, also working as a guide, but that I also owned a new guide service. As if that wasn't evident from the speech I had just given. But I was like a schoolkid, very nervous; I felt like I hadn't ever talked with a girl so beautiful. I told her I was about to go out to the mountains to work for two weeks, but maybe I could get her number and we could meet up after I returned. She agreed.

That course seemed to take forever to finish. I was anxious to get back to civilization and see if Alexia even remembered me, let alone wanted to get together. Coincidentally it was my friend Diego who picked me up from the field, and I told him about my encounter with one of the students, Alexia, in his first-aid class. As we drove back to the city, I explained to him that Alexia and I were kind of flirting a bit, and I was about to text her to try to meet up. I remember him coaching me on the finer points crucial for talking to the transplanted Portenas from Buenos Aires living in Bariloche. Like a seasoned professional, Diego instructed me, "For these Argentina women, you have to be very direct. These girls are so used to getting hit on by men essentially every day, all day, that they have adapted to be standoffish and used to men getting straight to the point. At the end of your message, don't just say goodbye or 'hope to see you,' but instead, write 'Te mando un beso.' That translates to 'I send you a kiss.' This cuts right through any question about your interest in her."

His advice worked, and we met later that day at a patio overlooking the massive lake of Nahuel Huapi for a coffee. Again, the fact that I had an actual apartment there and offered to make us glasses of maté that afternoon gave me the inside cool points needed. We had a fantastic time and almost right away began dating. It was an enjoyable time, and I felt proud walking into a restaurant or shop and having the kind of girlfriend that turned every guy's head. Suddenly, I did not want to go back into the field as often as I used to. I was also trying my best to learn the nuances of Argentinean Spanish, with its multitude of slang and distinct accent compared to other Latin American countries.

Like many other foreigners who visit Argentina, I was beginning to think about relocating permanently there. I loved the vibrancy of the people, attending cookouts known as *asados*, drinking red wine, and cooking steaks on the red-hot coals from the fire on the ground. We drank maté, took hikes in the mountains, and fumbled our way through a mix of Spanglish as I tried to pick up the more subtle accent of the Castellano. Alexia told me there are only two ways you can learn Spanish: "in the cradle or in the bed." You were born in Argentina or had to marry a girl from there.

With a new relationship and my budding guiding career, I was on top of the world. I had done my best to convince Alexia that I only had to go to Pakistan for a short climb that upcoming summer, and I would be back in no time.

My drive to climb and travel had not abated. I had sent my résumé to a company in Australia that was planning to lead a trip to attempt both

K2 and Broad Peak in Pakistan (the story told in the Prologue). When I left Alexia to follow that passion, the relationship worked for a while. But as is often the case, things were not that simple. I was learning something that most guides discover in life—dating while trying to juggle a mountain guide life is hard. She eventually got tired of waiting and broke it off.

I was heartbroken, wondering if I would ever have a girlfriend if I had this uncontrollable urge to take adventure trips all over the world. It foreshadowed several more relationships that would ultimately become strained because of yet another Himalayan trip to Pakistan or Nepal. I figured I would need to find a balance between loving the mountains and loving a partner at some point. I learned this lesson the hard way, and always remembered a quote from a friend in Bariloche that described perfectly that first experience with Alexia: "A girl like that doesn't sleep alone."

In June 2006, I made my way for the first time to the mighty Karakoram Himalayan mountains in Pakistan. I was hired by the Australian company as the assistant leader of a non-guided expedition doubleheader to try to climb Broad Peak and K2. It was commercially organized, but the team members were expected to be highly experienced individuals who did not require a guided trip but wanted all the logistics and leadership handled. Jeff Justman, one of my co-workers at RMI, was the expedition leader. JJ, as he was known in mountain circles, had just finished guiding on Everest. I had just climbed Cho Oyu and was flying into Pakistan from Nepal to meet the team.

My introduction to Pakistan was fitting of the times. In 2006 there was quite a lot of hesitation for Westerners to travel to that part of the world, mainly due to the US/Iraq war and the conflicts among Islamic states. I had some trepidation about this aspect of the trip, but I was frankly more concerned with trying to climb K2.

During my flight from Kathmandu, I was caught in an extended flight delay through New Delhi and had an epic introduction to traveling in Pakistan. When I finally landed in Islamabad in the middle of the night, a full two days behind schedule, the team had already departed in the bus toward the Karakoram Highway. I called my handler at the company from a pay phone outside the airport. He simply told me to catch a bus to some small town along the way where a taxi would be waiting for me. I took an overnight small van packed with about twenty-five other locals and me, the lone foreigner, with my North Face duffle bags on my lap, crammed in the back. I was dropped off at a middle-of-nowhere bus station. My "taxi" turned out to be a motorcycle that I was supposed to jump on while my bags were put into a car, which made no sense to me, but hey, it's an adventure. These guys dropped me off in the middle of what seemed like the desert, at the intersection of two roads, where I waited for thirty minutes by myself staring into the unknown. Finally, remarkably, the bus with my team pulled up, and I jumped on board with a sense of relief to meet the team.

That trip was another learning experience. Since JJ and I were already acclimated from our respective climbs in Nepal and Tibet, we focused on fixing ropes on Broad Peak so that the team members could come behind and climb the route. It was amazing. I was not getting paid for the trip, but my expedition was fully funded in exchange for helping to lead the trip. This fell right in line with my philosophy of making things happen for myself and taking chances to gain opportunities.

The Broad Peak part of the expedition went quite well, even with so many team members. JJ and I acted somewhat like expedition leaders, holding meetings and managing the local staff of high-altitude porters, but we were free to climb ahead of the group. Our focus was on making the route, organizing the camps, and fixing rope. We did not need to guide anyone, which was quite a liberating feeling.

Since we were efficient and had good luck with the weather, it only took about three weeks to be in a position to make a summit attempt. JJ and I and three high-altitude porters made our way to set up a high camp and make a run at the summit.

The morning was perfect, deep blue skies in every direction, with sunshine and only a hint of wind brushing off the top of Gasherbrum 4's shining wall to the south. I was at home, so to speak, completely alone on one of the classic mountains in the Karakoram. I was in my element, climbing along the knife-edge rock and ice ridge of 8,188-meter Broad Peak, the twelfth-highest mountain on earth. The old, semi-deteriorated rope that had been fixed years before by previous expeditions stretched out ahead but began to disappear into past seasons of snowfall, sun, and wind. The seemingly never-ending narrow rock and ice passage to the summit stretched into the spindrift-filled air, and I remember looking forward to each vertical foot of climbing, eager to discover what lay ahead. The margin for error was slim in this kind of climbing, with an unwelcome fate down 3,000-foot vertical drops on the fluted snow slope to the east and a similarly distressing outcome of any potential misstep down the more-rocky, windswept, western face.

I was all alone due to the amount of extremely difficult post-holing and step-kicking our small summit push team had endured. JJ and the porters had turned back earlier at a prominent col between the two massive independent summit features. They were descending to the relative safety of our high camp, which consisted of two single-wall nylon tents and a few propane gas stoves, dug into the side of a steep snow slope. JJ had felt sick and was battling a stomach infection. Our three Pakistani high-altitude porters had decided to turn back for their own reasons, most likely fueled by the apprehension of the unknown. On the other hand, I felt strong, and the weather was stable. So with K2 standing proud at the head of the valley and the massive Baltoro Glacier snaking away like an icy highway down the valley floor below, I had decided to press on alone toward the summit.

Some thoughts began to creep into my head as I climbed farther and farther away from the relative safety of our tiny high camp thousands of feet below. What if the weather took a turn for the worse? A whiteout could come at any time, and my footsteps could get blown in with snow. What if I cannot retrace the route or get injured up here, left to lie and wonder why I love playing this dangerous game? I had to revert to being a climber, a mountaineer, and dial all that back, along with thoughts about the massive exposure and climbing unroped and alone on unforgiving terrain.

I constantly reminded myself to make good ice axe and crampon placements, and to breathe. My head was foggy due to the extremely high altitude (I was not using supplemental oxygen). Still, I found a rhythm, and several hours began to melt away as I got closer to Broad Peak's elusive high point. It is a summit located on a seemingly arbitrary high ridge of rock and snow in one of the greatest mountain ranges on the planet. The ice in my beard grew thick with the moisture of each exhale at over 26,000 feet and minus 20 degrees. Suddenly I remembered to enjoy this, to take in the position. The summit ridge of Broad Peak is notoriously long, with several false summits along the way, but I was determined to continue until the narrow horizon gave way to the highest point. Climbing in the sun alone for several hours on a striking ridge higher than 26,000 feet to the summit of a Himalayan giant can only be described as one of my most fantastic memories. All to reach the highest point where there was no more uphill. This was one of those fleeting moments when I experienced the sensation and warm glow of success and accomplishment, and felt good about my chosen pursuit.

Broad Peak was my fourth summit of an 8,000-meter peak. Three of those were without the use of supplemental oxygen. Only on Everest had I used oxygen. The Broad Peak success would soon become juxtaposed with my next month in the Karakoram as the final piece of my larger goal to personally try to reach the summit of three 8,000-meter mountains back to back to back. As a team, we still had our eyes on K2, the second-highest mountain in the world and one of the more challenging high peaks to summit.

Even though I had just climbed two 8,000-meter mountains within the previous month—Cho Oyu in Tibet, the sixth-highest mountain in the world at 26,906 feet, and now Broad Peak, I felt good. Climbing three of these giants in a row seemed like a perfectly normal course of action for me at the time. I was in my early thirties, still with no family commitments, and armed with the motivating broken heart from the breakup with Alexia. My insatiable thirst for climbing the highest peaks in the world's great mountain ranges was only growing. I would spend another month in the Karakoram, working with my team and climbers from other international expeditions to fix ropes and stock successively higher camps on the Abruzzi Ridge route of the infamous K2 before ultimately making the decision to turn back on that objective (described in the Prologue).

When we got back to Skardu, I checked my email in the lodge and found two very exciting messages. The previous summer, while working on Mount Rainier, I had met Christine Boskoff in Seattle. Christine was an accomplished high-altitude mountaineer at the time, with the most 8,000-meter summits of any female, and she was the owner of Mountain Madness. She had taken over the reins after Scott Fisher passed away on Everest in the 1996 disaster.

Mountain Madness was in a transition phase regarding leadership for their Everest program. I had met with Christine last summer to offer my résumé and see if there was any chance of Himalayan work in the future. The company I was already working for, RMI, had only been hinting at a possible return to Everest commercially. I was merely looking at all avenues of potential work.

The first email was from Christine, offering the opportunity to guide their expedition to Everest the following spring. Just a few emails down, another was from Peter Whittaker, the principal owner of RMI. He told me they were planning to organize two Everest trips for the upcoming season. One would be led by Ed Viesturs, with Jeff Justman as the second guide; the other group would be led by Brent Okita, and I was offered the spot as the second guide.

It was a surreal position for me to be in. Not that long ago, I had decided to give up my career as a geologist and pursue my passion headlong. Now here I was with offers from Mountain Madness *and* Rainier Mountaineering to work on Everest.

I took a family vacation to my brother Tate's house in Miami and pondered the intricacies of my decision with my parents. They probably did not grasp the magnitude of the opportunities but offered advice nonetheless. In the end I decided to accept the RMI offer because I wanted to remain loyal to the company I was already working for. Turns out it was the wrong decision because RMI did not get enough clients signed up for their trips to operate on Everest that year. Mountain Madness did.

One day during the spring of 2007, Peter Whittaker wanted to talk out on the lawn of the Ashford base camp for RMI. He explained that they were planning to run a trip to Cho Oyu, the mountain I had already guided twice, where I made both ascents without the use of supplemental oxygen. Peter offered me the role of leading the expedition and guiding the trip along with Casey Grom. I always thought that Casey felt slighted by me getting the lead role. He had many more years guiding with RMI and was a very competent expedition leader, and even had Everest on his résumé. But I assumed it was because I had already been to Cho Oyu twice that I had the asterisk next to my name.

I was really psyched. My autumn was booked. Since I had worked two full summers on Rainier, I had enough leverage to ask Peter if I could miss out on the 2007 summer to lead an expedition for that same Australian company I went to K2 and Broad Peak for. He agreed that more Himalayan leading experience was good for his guides to have. And so I said yes to Gasherbrum 2. At 26,358 feet, G2 is the thirteenth-highest mountain on the planet, again located in the Karakoram of Pakistan.

Up to this point, I had had a lot of success on 8,000-meter peaks, and I felt like I had momentum. The thought of eventually going for all fourteen of the 8,000-meter peaks began to creep into my subconscious at this stage, but it was not a goal. I had always wanted to climb Gasherbrum 2 for some reason, and this was the perfect opportunity. This time I was getting a salary for leading the trip, and my cachet for leading Himalayan expeditions was slowly building. I asked Dave Elmore to go along as the assistant expedition leader, and he agreed. We did not have a pressing schedule yet at Mountain Professionals, so we were free to take opportunities like this to further our own objectives.

The expedition for the first half of the trip was mostly uneventful, other than having to kick one of our climbers off the trip because he kept insisting he did not have to be roped up to his rope team while traveling through a dangerous icefall and crevasse section. The final straw came one morning at base camp when our liaison officer informed me that said climber had woken in the middle of the night and followed another team most of the way to Camp One, alone and unroped, while our team slept in base camp. It was an easy decision to make. He was putting himself and other people at enormous risk, and I made the decision to send him packing back to Skardu.

That season on G2 had been plagued with epically lousy weather. We were spending a week at a time between rotations to the higher camps, stuck in base camp due to massive snowfall events. It was getting late in the climbing season, and we had only established Camp Two at 21,300 feet. The avalanche hazard on the slopes above had been a major road-block to all the teams trying to climb the mountain that year.

Our team mainly worked alongside the guides from Amical, a German outfitter; a small Mountain Madness expedition team led by Phil Crampton, the founder of Altitude Junkies; and Jaime McGuinness of Project Himalaya. Phil had become a good friend of mine over the years on many expeditions in the Himalayas. Dave and I mostly talked with him about working together on a possible summit push if the weather ever presented an opportunity.

As the days melted away and time on the permit got tight, many of the climbing teams felt the itch to try for a summit attempt before the summer season came to a close. There had been a recent three-day snowfall event on the mountain, and the best thing to do was wait and let that snow settle. Or better yet, avalanche the slopes before you go up and roll the dice. After waiting for two full days, I and another climber ascended to Camp One, figuring we would give the more-loaded slope above Camp Two an extra day to do whatever it was going to do. Then we would tentatively climb above Camp Two at 21,325 feet to see if it was viable to make an attempt at reaching Camp Three, which was located at 22,966 feet.

The Amical commercial group was one day ahead of us, having decided to go pretty soon after the snow event toward the upper camps. They had a very experienced guide as an expedition leader. Still, I remember thinking it was a bit early to go up. On July 18, 2007, after a perfect afternoon of climbing, my partner and I reached the Camp Two tents and settled in to relax. We wanted to get a feel of what the mountain was saying. Phil and his group were about an hour behind our group, still on the way up to Camp Two. We could see the Amical group of about six climbers stretched out on the route heading to Camp Three above us when a massive crack sounded. In retrospect, we believe Dirk Groeger, the guide for Amical, tried to free the buried fixed rope for his clients, which may have triggered the event. The whole slope seemed to give way, and with it, the entire group of climbers. I can recall the sickening feeling as I watched several people tumble in the slide. Two guys simply disappeared over a huge drop. Three climbers who were fighting for their lives in the rushing snow came to a stop on the mountain face to the right and about 200 meters above Camp Two, and the last climber on the team was nowhere to be seen.

In these scenarios, your adrenaline begins to pulse right away. Our team and some of the other climbers in camp immediately put on our climbing gear to traverse out on the snow slope and try to get to the three injured climbers that were visibly alive. Their guide, Dirk, was barely buried in the snow and managed to get out on his own with only an arm injury. However, the other two climbers were in worse shape and needed immediate help. They were an Austrian and an already famous Japanese high-altitude climber named Hirotaka Takeuchi (Hiro), who had ascended something like ten 8,000-meter peaks by the time of the accident. Both the Austrian and Hiro were in terrible shape with internal trauma.

A Swiss climber named Walo, a doctor, went to save the Austrian while we tried to stabilize Hiro. Walo administered CPR to the Austrian climber, who was slipping away rapidly and unfortunately died during the frenzied attempt to save him.

Our attention as a collective group of rescuers then turned to Hiro. Several of us banded together to get him over to the Camp Two tents and off the dangerous slope. As late afternoon approached, I knew we needed to act fast if we were going to save his life. I began radio communication with Dave in our base camp as a communication line between the mountain, base camp, and Skardu. We needed a helicopter and fast.

Working with the liaison officers, the base camp team managed to organize a helicopter rescue out of Skardu. They sent up word to the rescue team that a chopper would arrive in about two hours, so we needed to do our best to make a helipad. This is not an easy task at 21,000 feet on the side of a mountain. Still, the whole group of climbers pitched in with shovels and feet, and we cleared a flat area and marked a large "H" in the snow with drink mix from water bottles.

We packaged up Hiro as best as we could with sleeping pads and slings and hoped for a speedy arrival of the chopper. When eventually the whacking of blades could be heard off in the distance, we all felt a sense of relief. We had no idea what the rescue helicopter's plan was. Could they land, or would they long line him? The first pass was just a scouting mission by the pilot. He maneuvered the army helicopter to within about a hundred feet of our location, the prop wash blasting us. We could see the would-be rescuers in the open cargo area. But after an hour of circling the rescue site, they tailed off and headed back down the valley.

I talked with Dave again at base camp; he informed me that the helicopter had landed back in base camp to off-load an officer to make the chopper as light as possible. They were going to make another attempt, but the pilot would not be able to land. Instead, the hovering helicopter would lower a rescue sled, and we would try to grab it as it was dragged across the snowy slopes. Then we would need to quickly clip Hiro into the sled while holding it as steady as possible. This made us all very nervous, to say the least.

On the second attempt, we were amped up and ready to get Hiro off the mountain. When the helicopter approached our location, hovering just off a steep drop at the edge of Camp Two, we could see the officer in the back open the cargo door and signal that he was about to drop the rescue sled out of the helicopter. In nervous anticipation, we got ready and made final plans about who would do which little task. When the officer pushed the sled out of the cargo bay door, we watched with a sickening feeling as it dropped 2,000 feet into the void. It had not been clipped to the cable.

That was it. The rescue group was devastated emotionally. The chopper turned down the valley, and we somberly watched it make its way toward Skardu. There would be no helicopter rescue that night. The information coming in from base camp was that the helicopter might return tomorrow, but Hiro needed to be moved down to Camp One. Otherwise they could not retrieve him.

We moved Hiro into my tent and made a plan with the various "rescue" team members, who were all just climbers doing the right thing of their own free will to assist a fellow climber. Finally, in a herculean effort, a German climber named Helmut descended all the way to Camp One and returned to Camp Two that evening, bringing crucial oxygen to help keep Hiro alive through the night.

That entire evening, Mark Sheen and I took turns lying in the tent with Hiro as he coughed and winced in pain. There were many moments when I thought he would die right there. Often he would stop breathing altogether, and one of us would have to rush to awaken him. It was terrifying. Hirotaka's English was limited, and I remember over and over asking him the same simple questions to try to keep him alert.

The next morning a collective group of climbers, guides, clients, and porters pitched in and spent the day making anchors in the snow, lowering Hiro pitch by pitch down the rugged terrain. Finally, after a grueling day for everyone involved, we managed to get him safely down to Camp One. The helicopter was able to land on flat snow at 19,300 feet in elevation. When Hiro was whisked off en route for Skardu, all the rescuers, from many nationalities and backgrounds, gave one another high fives and hugs and celebrated. We would later find out that Hiro had sustained a broken back, a collapsed lung, and many other internal injuries in the avalanche fall. However, he survived and made a full recovery.

Four years later, on the slopes of Mount Dhaulagiri, I met Hiro once again. Conversing in our broken English, I told him I had been with him in the tent that night on Gasherbrum 2. He joyfully let out a big laugh and hugged me. Hirotaka Takeuchi would go on to finish climbing all fourteen 8,000-meter peaks, the first Japanese person to do so. That made me happy, knowing he recovered and continued to follow his passion.

The entire month of August, I tried to patch up my relationship with Alexia back in Argentina. Things were good for a while, and then not so much. I was leaving for Cho Oyu in September to lead the trip for RMI. I finally "got the message" from Alexia that we were finished. I traveled too much, so what was the point? I understood her feelings, but it still hurt. I was heartbroken the whole Cho Oyu trip, but I remained professional. Deep down, I was in pain. Even though I was only in my mid-thirties, I felt like I would never find another meaningful relationship again. I received wisdom from Phil Crampton, who was leading his Mountain Madness expedition, and even talked to his wife for the female perspective on relationships and guiding. The small circle of professional adventurers can be a sound support system.

For the trip, RMI had contracted with Himex, Russell Brice's company, to handle the logistics. It is safe to say that Russell has become legendary in Himalayan circles over his vast career. A very competent and successful climber turned guide, he had slowly transitioned into running his expeditions from base camp and letting his guides do the on-mountain work. I had only met him a couple of times in passing during my previous Tibetan expeditions and had always felt both reverence and a little bit of self-serving jealousy, as he was considered a beacon of Himalayan leadership. As I got to know him more on a personal level, that feeling disappeared, and I simply respected his experience and judgment and tried to soak up information anytime I shared a bottle of scotch with him in a base camp somewhere.

Our all-male team had our interest piqued when we learned there would be an all-female Norwegian team sharing our base camp services. There also would be a twenty-girl Croatian expedition planning to camp next door to our location. This was highly uncharacteristic of Himalayan expeditions at the time; if you were a single woman in base camp, you had the interest of all the male-dominated camps. A pretty woman who was also a climber could get out of her tent at base camp, and it would look like a wild pack of meerkats popping up out of tents as every man in camp came out to get a glimpse. The competition was always on. But now, there would be thirty or more females in the base camp. I didn't care, though; I was still fretting over how I could lose Alexia, and feeling like the world had ended. So I just focused on my job leading another expedition to climb the sixth-highest mountain in the world—no small task.

After arriving at base camp, we moved in and got things sorted with our clients. Russell told Casey and me that we should come to the guide meeting for cocktails at four that afternoon. Like I said before, it is often the people you remember about a trip, and I was about to have one of those connections you never forget. The moment I walked into the guide's tent, at the end of a small table surrounded by burly mountain guides in thick down jackets, I saw these piercing blue eyes nestled under a big mop of curly hair. They belonged to the stunning Cecilie Skog, a tanned Norwegian beauty. I was shocked, almost speechless. We were introduced, and I found out she was the leader of the Norwegian team.

We quickly became friends over the next few days, once I recovered from my awkward first moment. She was a hell of a climber and fun to hang out with.

That season on Cho Oyu was challenging from a weather standpoint. It snowed an incredible amount, and there were several camps on the mountain that got torched by winds. I was guiding a group for RMI and had the lead role for my team, but I relied on Russell and his decision-making with his staff regarding the mountain logistics. Unfortunately, in the end, the mountain was not going to host climbers that year. Russell eventually decided the objective risk from avalanches was too significant, and he pulled the plug on the expedition. It was a tough pill to swallow as a guide team.

Casey and I could not really do anything to change the outcome, and we left the mountain without a summit. However, we did make great relationships. My eyes were opened to the polar ski world of North and South Pole expeditions through conversations with Cecilie at base camp over tea. The whole notion of the True Adventurers Grand Slam had been introduced to me there. Cecilie was the only female in the world to accomplish it. So I left that trip, gaining more experience and judgment, but no summit.

In the spring of 2008, I guided our Mountain Professionals Everest trip, and we had a successful year, but after summiting, I frostbit my toe (as explained in the Prologue). This dashed my plans to go back to K2 that summer. I had my name on a permit and had already purchased the plane ticket, but was forced to back out. The story of the 2008 K2 disaster is well documented in books like *No Way Down* by Graham Bowley and several documentaries.

I would have been right there, most likely on the same summit day as the rest of the climbers trapped above the bottleneck at 27,000 feet. Instead, I was in my room in Boulder, Colorado, peeling off black skin from my toe as it healed from frostbite. I was following the updates online and getting minute-by-minute messages from friends about the status of trapped climbers in the Death Zone. Throughout that sleepless night, I frantically wrote emails to my expedition partners who were there. I sent an email to Cecilie's address, knowing that it may never be read. She was up there on the summit push with her husband Rolf and Lars Nessa. I simply wrote, "Please get down safely. There are many people who care about you." The ice serac, which collapsed that night, took Cecilie's husband as she watched.

My friends Ger McDonnell and Wilco Van Rooijen, with whom I had attempted K2 in 2006, were above the bottleneck that night. Ger would die on K2. Wilco miraculously made it down after a desperate bivouac in the Death Zone and suffered bad frostbite injuries on his feet but survived. Many other acquaintances and colleagues were there on that day. For whatever reason the universe had for me, I was not.

Several months later, in the fall of 2008, I was ready for a break from travel. My old boss at the geology firm I had worked for contacted me to see if I was interested in one last fieldwork project. I always loved being back in Mississippi, where I had lived for years while getting my university degree at Ole Miss. It seemed like a nice change of pace to go back and be normal for a few weeks, away from all the climbing drama. On the last day of my fieldwork in the small town whose name I don't even remember now, I was sitting in a small coffee shop reading emails. I had a message from Cecilie. I had not heard anything from her since the accident on K2.

Anxious to talk to her, we quickly agreed to do a Skype video call. I had a strange feeling of excitement mixed with sorrow. I did not know how to talk to her about the accident and her loss, but I felt special. Cecilie Skog not only remembered me as a friend but also wanted to reach out. There, sitting in small-town southern USA, I was pulled back into my circles of adventure and logged into the call.

CHAPTER FIVE

Seventy Days of Light

SOMETIMES IN LIFE, CHANGE HAPPENS SLOWLY. OVER TIME THE PATH you are on builds momentum. Things start to happen, and before you realize it, suddenly everything is different. But sometimes, change occurs in the spur of the moment. The latter happened to me sitting in a funky little coffee shop in Boulder with Cecilie one sunny December day. There was snow covering the ground from a recent storm, but the air outside was warming the town on a fine Front Range day. We were sitting across from each other sipping from steaming mugs when she casually mentioned, "I think I may try to ski across Antarctica sometime; I want to ski from Berkner Island to the other side."

She had been struggling to deal with her understandable depression and had taken me up on an offer to visit me in Colorado. Trying to sort out why her husband was killed on a mountain while she was spared had been taking its toll on her. She was confused and trying to move the puzzle pieces of why this tragedy had occurred into a discernible picture. She confided in close friends that she had not wanted to leave the mountain. She could have just stayed up there forever near her companion. Thankfully, she had been encouraged by her climbing partners, especially Lars Nessa, to find the strength to descend and go on with life.

Stuck back home for months in Stavanger, in northern Norway, the rainy autumn weather had worn her down. She felt trapped in her own mind and by the media, who were interested in knowing about her story and her progression through the aftermath of the tragedy. So she had decided to take a break. Coming to visit me seemed like as good an escape as any.

We planned a road trip to go ice climbing in the town of Ouray, deep in the Colorado Rockies, because it was something she loved to do. I thought this would take her mind off the entire situation, but it had the exact opposite outcome. Being on a frozen waterfall with the possibility of falling chunks of ice and snow wasn't a good thing. It triggered bad memories and brought her back to K2, the last place she wanted to revisit. So we ditched the idea of climbing altogether and flew to New York City. We figured a bit of retail therapy might be just the contradictory scene for a few brief moments of escape. It was a peaceful time, and I tried to act like a supportive friend to someone in need. After a fun couple days, we headed back West.

Relaxing back in Boulder, we started exchanging stories about our times in the wild. I was fascinated as she told me about all the amazing experiences she had already been through at this point in her life. Her experiences were in a different realm than mine had been. I climbed mountains while guiding clients to the top. She had crossed huge ice fields and undertook epic expeditions.

She told me about going on these polar ski expeditions, such as the unsupported North Pole trip, and how expensive it could be. It seemed like raising money for the trips had always been hard work, just as it is for everyone, but relatively straightforward at this point in her career since she was established as an outdoor figure in Norway. However, when she and Rolf went to the North Pole or K2, the budgets were in the stratosphere, dwarfing the amounts I had previously thought of as monumental in my career.

I, on the other hand, had been working as a guide making a meager income while trying to tick off faraway goals. Working for free or little pay was my norm. I might try to scratch together a few small-time sponsorships from some semi-interested sources to help pay for part of a plane ticket, but that was the limit of my fundraising experience. Her mindset was in a whole other dimension. Having conversations about her past expeditions opened my eyes to budgets north of $200,000 for a North Pole trip: "Yeah, we raised it, and when we got picked up by a helicopter that had extra space to share in the end, we even made that little portion of the money back in profit." Or $100,000 for a K2 expedition: "Of course, we had twenty extra porters to bring in all the good food from home, extra tents, and bean bag chairs for base camp." As opposed to my K2 attempt in 2006, when I had volunteered to work for two months leading people on the expedition in exchange for a chance to climb it in any form or fashion. I had climbed some peaks by this point, but she was a whole different league of adventurer. She made big ideas seem normal and within reach.

So when she mentioned crossing Antarctica, it only took me a moment to blurt out, "I will go with you if you want." She took a few seconds to absorb my instant response, careful not to offer up an immediate opportunity. Besides the fact that it was not yet a real trip, only a dream, she also had to think about potentially dragging along a mountaineer in Antarctica. Looking back, I do believe she had confidence in me as a potential partner on the expedition; otherwise she would not have mentioned the idea to me in the first place. We agreed in theory to move forward with the plan to pursue the trip. However, if it became a realistic proposition, I would need to make considerable strides in learning the required skills for an epic polar ski traverse.

At that scratched-up and slightly wobbly coffee table in Boulder, far from her home in Norway, she decided to take a chance with a marginally experienced partner instead of a polar superstar. The dream for our journey was born from a true passion for adventure in the purist style—to travel under human power across the most pristine landscape on earth and complete the first unsupported/unassisted (no resupplies or kites) ski traverse of the Antarctica landmass.

Cecilie and Rolf had talked in the past about a potential expedition that followed this unique route she had mentioned. It was one that only a few in a small circle of polar explorers would even understand the significance of, crossing the vast white, windswept terrain of Antarctica alone and unaided. They had already skied the more traditional route on an unsupported trip from Hercules Inlet to the South Pole, so they knew the rigor such an expedition posed.

Rolf had accomplished an amazingly long and difficult kite-ski journey across Antarctica with another partner, one of the longest-distance trips in history. But he and Cecilie had discussed the potential to ski, unaided by kites or resupply drops, from Berkner Island in the Weddell Sea to the South Pole and then across to the Ross Sea side of the continent, with the ultimate goal of reaching the US base of McMurdo. Essentially it would be trying to reproduce the route accomplished by Borge Ousland during his record-breaking 1996–1997 first solo unsupported crossing of Antarctica. Borge had used a kite for some portions of the journey, which to purists was termed assisted at the time. The idea was to attempt to replicate the route but without any use of kites.

Even after the loss of Rolf, that dream was still alive, and I could sense it was maybe a feeling of owing it to him that motivated Cecilie to try to make the trip. But I also think it meant something to her, a chance to heal doing something she loved in a special place.

A crucial part of my agreement with Cecilie from the beginning was that I would have to learn how to ski across polar landscapes. It makes sense, right? She was putting a lot of trust in my abilities as an expedition partner and my background on climbing trips. On that, I was solid, but she was not about to risk such a big goal on an American without polar ski experience.

In March 2009, Cecilie devised a plan to go back to Greenland and do an east to west ski traverse with her friends. I was invited to go along as a personal polar shakedown. I was excited about the prospect of being a student again and learning how to ski in this fashion. When we made a short training trip in the mountains of Norway beforehand, she knew she had her work cut out for her. I had skied downhill often enough, but strapping skinny polar skis on my feet was a different ball game; I looked like a newborn foal trying to walk. To this day, she still gets a laugh out of audiences during her speeches back home. The slides of the non-Norwegian lying in the snow on failed attempts to overcome obstacles that Norwegians deal with from the time they are infants make her audiences chuckle.

I tried my best to swallow my pride. I marveled at the Scandinavians on the trip; it seemed like they were born with skis on their feet. I was immersed in a full-time school as I labored across Greenland with Cecilie, her two girlfriends Silje Hanum Padøy and Linn Yttervik, and her manager Bjørn Sekkesæter. They were pros and appreciated my enthusiasm on the snow. I learned how to manage my time on these types of expeditions, improved my ski techniques, and developed a healthy dose of self-deprecating knowledge about how little I knew.

It was a challenging expedition in many ways. Still, it was exactly what I needed to prepare for the upcoming Antarctica crossing. It also helped Cecilie work through some of the early psychological hurdles of losing Rolf on K2.

Not long after I returned to Boulder from that trip, I had a chance encounter with someone who would play a significant role in the future.

My friend Doug Sandok, who had let me live in his basement off and on for years and with whom I had instructed mountaineering courses in Patagonia, invited me to a slide presentation he was giving at Sherpa's Restaurant in Boulder. He had also invited a guy named Eric Larsen. Doug thought we should meet, and introduced me to him that evening. I knew who Eric was from his status as a polar explorer and past expeditions he had completed in the Arctic. My adventure world expanded.

Eric had recently moved to Boulder to be closer to his then-girlfriend, now wife, Maria Hennessey. He was in the middle of planning an extraordinary project in which he would try to climb Mount Everest and ski coast to Pole expeditions to both the North and South Poles—all within a year. He called the project "Save the Poles," referring to the earth's three poles—north and south and the highest point. Any one of these trips would be quite an accomplishment as a stand-alone expedition, but to do all three in one calendar year would require a masterful choreography of logistics and fundraising. The trouble was that Eric had not climbed much so was looking for a way to bone up on his mountaineering skills.

Doug figured I was more of a mountaineer, but since I had skied across Greenland and was tentatively planning to ski across Antarctica, he figured I was kind of into polar stuff. Eric was an accomplished polar adventurer but needed to find mountain climbing outlets to get additional advice and experience to try to climb Everest. It was an instant match for future trips.

I talked with Eric a lot and learned more about his project. I wanted to climb Denali, so I pitched him the idea of going that year with me and another climbing buddy from Pakistan, Mark Sheen. It would be an excellent way to get him dialed for Everest and an opportunity for me to climb the mountain. I also told Eric that I would either go with him to Everest or organize his trip with my staff in Nepal to help with cost savings.

Realizing that Eric would be in the Arctic for a full-length ski trip to the North Pole most of the spring 2010 season, we needed to organize an autumn climb on Everest. I knew I was already going to be on another mountain, so I would not be able to join him on that autumn trip. Still, I felt confident that our Sherpa crew could manage the climb with Eric since he had so much expedition experience in the polar world. We set about making all these plans in earnest.

In July we took off for Denali, meeting Mark in Talkeetna. We got delayed a few days before flying to Muldrow Glacier, but things happened fast once we got out there. We traveled efficiently along the West Buttress lower route, without caches or back carries of gear, because all three of us were pretty fit and moving fast. It was an interesting time because Eric and I were sizing each other up on clothing, gear, travel, and so on. Eric still likes to remind me of the time on the trip when he commented about the layering system I had personally chosen for the morning. My response to him was simply, "Don't worry about me." It is our nature to question things like this as guides, so we just laughed about it.

We arrived at the 14,000-foot camp three days after landing at the glacier airstrip. We took one rest day; the plan was to head higher the next day to ferry supplies to the base of the ridge at 16,000 feet to cache for a high camp.

We left camp very early that morning and climbed rapidly to the "16 ridge." The weather was unbelievably perfect, with no wind and blue skies in every direction. When we set down our loads of gear, we all felt great. We must have been thinking the same thing; I just said it first. I looked at everyone and said, "Do you guys want to just keep going to the summit?"

It took about one minute of discussion before we all agreed. We felt great, the weather was perfect, so why not try for the summit? It was an ideal day, and we reached the summit by mid-afternoon. All of us were beaming as we stood together at the top.

We descended back to the 14,000-foot camp by evening and crashed after such a long day. We were totally psyched to have climbed Denali so quickly and easily. We had been blessed with fantastic weather, which is not always the case there. On the walk out to the ski-equipped plane that would pick us up on the Muldrow Glacier, I had time to reflect on the experience and enjoy the fact that I had now climbed four of the Seven Summits. Only Mount Vinson in Antarctica, Mount Elbrus in Europe, and the Carstensz Pyramid in Indonesia remained.

As we rode in a hired transfer back to Anchorage to return to Colorado, Eric and I talked a lot about his upcoming Save the Poles project. Things were moving forward on his polar trips, and we had most of his logistics arranged for the autumn Everest climb. He was building his team for the North Pole portion of the overall project, and by now, he and I had a pretty strong rapport. He knew my only polar experience was skiing across Greenland, but also that I was planning to cross Antarctica next. That was enough for him to invite me to join his team on the North Pole ski trip from Cape Discovery, Canada, to the North Pole, in the spring of 2010.

It would be a supported trip, meaning there would be resupply drops of food and fuel at around three locations. My interest was in someday trying it unsupported, the same way my Antarctica trip with Cecilie was being planned. But I figured there might never be another opportunity to go on a full-length coast to North Pole trip, so we penciled me in on the spot.

That summer, back home in Colorado, I mulled over my evolving feelings for Cecilie. For me, it was becoming something more than a friendship; I was starting to have feelings for her. I felt them developing inside me, but I did not want to overstep my boundaries and jeopardize our relationship. She was still in the mourning process.

I also realized that in Norway, Cecilie was always in the public eye. Walking around, people would recognize her and say hello. She was a celebrity in her part of the world and would be conscious of the media picking up on a new relationship, even if one had not developed yet. So I remained focused on the expedition planning and secretly hoped that our time together might one day evolve into something more.

In the fall of 2009, I moved to Norway to train and prepare for the Antarctica crossing. It was still easy to pick up and live in another country at this point in my life because of my status as a "dirtbag" guide. I had few possessions other than expedition gear and climbing equipment in a dozen duffle bags and a P.O. box as a home address.

The two of us dove into preparations for our Antarctica trip. The clock was ticking, and we didn't think about much else. Cecilie was primarily in charge of wrangling for funding since she had good connections with the Norwegian media and gear companies. Polar ski expeditions hardly register at all in the United States, though this is changing with social media and climate change topics, but in Norway they are front-page news. We arranged several meetings with newspapers, television stations, and equipment companies to try to build excitement around our plan for a record-breaking Antarctica expedition. We also had numerous conversations with such polar luminaries as Borge Ousland, Sur Modre, and Lars Ebbesen, who were immensely helpful, provided feedback on our plans, and supplied aerial photographs, valuable advice, and practical tips to accomplish such an arduous undertaking.

Money always loomed large in our consciousness. The expedition budget was huge, and we knew that the clock was ticking to raise enough funds to cover the massive cost of flights to the prospective start and end points on our route. In an attempt to save some cash, we decided to see if we could hitch a ride off Antarctica via ship. That way, we would only have to charter a flight into Berkner Island (our planned starting point). It would save the costs of booking a return flight across the continent back to the flight company's base at Patriot Hills. Other people had been able to pull it off, so I began to look into it. Weeks of research went into trying to find some sort of vessel that would be in the McMurdo Sound area roughly around the time we hoped to be finishing the crossing of Antarctica.

The roadblocks were obvious. There were only a handful of Antarctic ice-hardened cruise ships on the water. To complicate matters more, the ship would need to have a helicopter on board to provide coverage and possible rescue for us close to the coast. Plus, we didn't quite know for sure when we would finish. Welcome to the world of high-cost adventures at the Poles.

We were hoping that the option to finish at McMurdo Station might work out because then we could traverse the length of the Ross Ice Shelf, which lies frozen atop the sea, to end there. McMurdo Station is part of the United States Antarctic Program located on the tip of Ross Island. While the scientists based there once welcomed adventurers with open arms, their receptions had started to cool. They had grown tired of feeling responsible for errant explorers that would suddenly arrive knocking on their door. That's how Rolf and his partner had exited Antarctica on their crossing, turning up in McMurdo hoping to arrange a fly-by-night escape on a passing ship. We knew better than to rely on the base for any help, so getting off Antarctica from there was a real logistical challenge.

Surprisingly, I found the perfect match. We entered into an agreement with a tourist ship that would be in McMurdo Sound around the time we would likely finish our crossing. It would have a helicopter on board, so if the vessel could not enter the bay due to pack ice, they would be able to fly to McMurdo to retrieve us. We could then take a leisurely cruise back to New Zealand. We liked the idea of sipping wine and eating steaks at the end of our trip. I booked a cabin and felt good to have knocked this issue out for us. Or at least I thought I had.

The lagging economy from the 2008 Great Recession was wreaking havoc with our plan. This delicate departure I had worked so hard to secure entirely came down to whether or not the tour company had enough paying passengers for that scheduled Antarctic cruise. After months of go or no-go anticipation, the company finally contacted us to report they had canceled the departure due to a lack of clients. The whole ship idea quickly sank. There would be no other options to get out from that side of Antarctica at the end of the summer season. So we came up with a much more expensive plan B.

Most commercial/expedition flights on Antarctica are run by Antarctic Logistics and Expeditions (ALE), which is the go-to flight operations company and the gateway for most private and commercial climbing and ski expeditions on the continent. It has developed such a seamless logistics package for explorers and tourists that it now assists in government contracts involving scientific projects. They even have shuttled the odd Royal family member to the South Pole for a visit.

A story within itself, ALE essentially came about as an idea while a group of mixed foreign adventurers were trekking on the north side of Mount Everest in the 1980s, and some of them wanted to get to Antarctica to climb. Over several decades, the band of hardened explorers managed to piece together an operation that could reliably fly and land a plane on the blue ice glacier of Patriot Hills.

Through a lot of time, energy, and financial struggle, ALE learned to run and manage the logistics with a military-like efficiency in the middle of Antarctica. The company essentially runs an airport on ice in minus-30 temperatures or worse. In November 2015, ALE was involved in the first landing of a commercial aircraft, a Boeing 737 Iceland Air plane, on the newer ice runway of Union Glacier. ALE subcontracts the airplanes and pilots from a Canadian company called Kenn Borek Air. Before each season, several pilots begin flying planes the length of the Americas from as far as the Arctic research stations in northern Canada. That migration can take up to two weeks in the smaller Twin Otter aircraft—all so that the planes will be ready for the relatively short Antarctic summer season.

As you can imagine, the logistics of travel in Antarctica are not cheap. To begin our journey, we chose a starting location that was both historical and personal for Cecilie. Berkner Island is a 17,000-square-mile ice rise over bedrock, located in the Ronne-Filchner Ice Shelf on the Weddell Sea. It was the general area in which Ernest Shackleton intended to start his Imperial Trans-Antarctic Expedition in 1914. The ice shelf east of the protruding arm of the Palmer Peninsula is where the epic story of the *Endurance* unfolded. When Shackleton's ship became entombed in sea ice, the crew rode out the winter in the boat. The boat slowly drifted before Shackleton and a few crewmen made a bold escape to South Georgia Island for help.

The Berkner Island start has a lot of significance for the small polar community of Norway. Besides being the starting point for Borge Ousland's first solo unsupported crossing of Antarctica in 1996, it had served as the starting point for another incredible Norwegian expedition.

Cato Zahl Pedersen skied to the South Pole from Berkner Island, along with Odd Harald Hauge and Lars Ebbesen. Cato is missing most of both lower arms, losing them in a childhood electrical wire accident, and is an inspirational figure in Norway for his feats.

Cecilie's husband Rolf had been a legend in the making on the polar ice caps. He came from the Norwegian old-school mentality where distance and suffering were a given, something to be expected and endured. Still, careful preparation and planning was also important and ran in their blood. This combination, along with extensive experience in the polar environment in a personal and leadership role, meant he was usually successful and always prepared. Rolf had grown up reading about the legendary Norwegian masters Roald Amundsen and Fritjof Nansen. He was establishing himself in the next wave of hardcore polar ski expedition heroes behind Børge and Rune Gjeldnes. It was mainly because of Rolf and Cecilie's original dream, and Børge's crossing route, that we decided to start on Berkner Island.

Our intention had always been to exit from the mainland down the Axel Heiberg Glacier, which holds particular significance in Antarctica as the entry point onto the Antarctica landmass for Amundsen's successful first expedition to the South Pole in 1910. So we knew there was a way to ski down from the mountains there and access the ice of the Ross Sea. We discussed this route at length with anyone who knew anything about that area. We also had photographs of the Axel Heiberg Glacier because this is where Rolf and his partner, Eirik Sønneland, had completed their kite crossing, which was then the world's longest ski journey, 2,360 miles long, taking 105 days to complete.

In discussions with ALE, we learned that our flights would cost $250,000. The dedicated flights for just the two of us and our equipment to such remote locations would require staging fuel in fifty-five-gallon drums ahead of time and using two different planes. A ski-equipped Twin Otter aircraft would deposit us at Berkner Island, and a larger aircraft with a greater range would pick us up on the Ross Ice Shelf. It was a daunting prospect, but they had total confidence that it would not be a problem. We committed to the tickets and moved on with our planning.

With the route determined, we could focus on several big pieces on the to-do list. We needed to do a lot of research and planning for two significant parts of the route: the access onto the Antarctica landmass proper at the Pensacola Mountains and the exit point down the Axel Heiberg Glacier. We also had to start collecting, cataloging, and packing all the gear and clothing for the trip. Funding was still an issue, mainly revolving around the massive flight bill.

The best way to go about tackling each task was to split up the work. I was having a heck of a time getting any interest in sponsorship funding from any American partners, even sponsors that I had worked with previously. Cecilie had many more promising leads in this department, so I took the lead on developing a sponsorship proposal. It was clean, straightforward, and relied on the idea of completing a crossing in the simplest manner. We did not want to make myriad promises such as providing photos and content in real-time or a dedicated website to draw followers. We were not even going to announce our objective until we were partway across the route.

This is in stark contrast to today's adventure world, one ruled by Instagram followers and Facebook likes. At that time, we were still in the transition of this shift in social media coverage. We had the old-school mentality of embarking on and completing a challenging journey and then bringing back the story of the accomplishment. We would not rely on constant updates to drum up interest, an approach that would not make it past the inbox of a marketing director today.

I believe this method of undertaking an expedition still has merit. It is imperative to focus solely on being in the place you are at mentally and physically when attempting a taxing expedition. Wasting time and energy focusing on constantly reporting what is going on to the outside world can drain you and tank an otherwise successful trip. Stay in the moment whenever possible.

We finally got some big breaks from Cecilie leveraging her contacts in Norway, where interest in this kind of trip runs high. Honestly, anything she did garnered attention. Bergans of Norway, the clothing and gear company that had supported Cecilie for several years, got behind the project with a promise of cold hard cash, plus the equipment we would need. We then parlayed that connection into others. In the world of sponsorships, once you land a major brand, others tend to start listening to you. Soon we were having many meetings.

The most important newspaper and the largest publishing company in Norway both got on board. The paper would have access to any updates we made via satellite phone calls and firsthand accounts, and the publisher would get a book written by Cecilie about the trip. More money and credibility were coming in, and we started to see that this thing could happen. I was able to get some other equipment companies to buy in for minor support, including gear. Money for our flights to and from southern Chile was donated by one of my first rock climbing partners, John Reiboldt, at Coker Capital Advisors. A theme of friends and family contributing to big goals was critical for this and future expeditions.

When STX Europe, a large shipbuilding company headquartered in Oslo, came to us with an offer for funding in exchange for a series of speeches given by Cecilie post-expedition, we knew we had the bulk of the financing needed to make the trip happen. In the end, Cecilie had to use some of her own money to subsidize the remaining balance, especially for the final payments. Yet another stress of large-scale and expensive polar expeditions is the financial strain of getting the money to operators before their deadlines, another fact of life I would experience in the future on later expeditions.

The expedition was due to start in just a few months, yet we were still working on both the entry and exit strategies. From conversations with Borge, we knew we would need to access the continent somewhere around Wujek Ridge after we had skied across the frozen Weddell Sea ice from Berkner Island. All we knew about the area was it had semi-steep slopes of snow and ice nestled between mountain peaks. The location was remote, and most of the terrain had been named by the US Geological Survey. Only scientists and flight crews had visited this part of the planet. So we needed maps and information. The USGS had the maps and the odd aerial photograph, but we needed firsthand knowledge too.

For that, we would need to visit Charles Swithinbank. Charles was a legendary Antarctica glaciologist who worked for the British Antarctic Survey at their headquarters in Cambridge, England. He was considered the premier Antarctica polar research glaciologist and had spent a long time studying the Pensacola Mountains area where we would be heading. Charles was a particular man and a scientist to the "T." We felt enormously lucky when he agreed to sit down with us and share his wisdom.

We flew to England and took the train to the Cambridge station. As the train whistle blew, we were met in the foggy nighttime air by an elderly gentleman in an English cap and cane. It was like a scene from an *Indiana Jones* film. We drove in his tiny car through the Cambridge streets to his home. His sparse kitchen was welcoming as he graciously offered us tea and smoked fish of some sort and then two beds in a guest room. After sharing a glass of brandy and hearing stories of crazy evenings spent with Russian scientists in some of the world's most remote locations, we retired to bed. The next day he laid out all his maps and photographs and gave us his opinion on routes. His information was in line with what we figured would be the most viable approach. Sitting with him, surrounded by old books and dusty globes, I felt like I was in another time, back when polar explorers were just beginning to venture into the frozen realms long closed to exploration. It was a special moment.

We spent about a week in Punta Arenas, Chile, preparing our equipment and packing food for our Antarctica trip. Ironically, Eric Larsen was also there, set to begin his Three Poles challenge by guiding the coast to the South Pole ski trip for ALE. It was good to have him to bounce ideas off, plus I was super excited for his journey.

As we boarded the plane bound for Antarctica, I mainly had nervous feelings mixed with pure excitement. The months before the expedition had been jammed with a flurry of to-do list sessions. Most of my nervous energy revolved around hoping we had everything dialed in and ready. When the Ilyushin Il-76 dropped us off on the Antarctic ice at the Patriot Hills camp, I was a bit in awe of everything we'd accomplished. The three months since sitting in Charles's study had screamed by in a frenzy of activity. We had shipped a mountain of gear to Chile ahead of our arrival, secured last-minute funding for the expedition costs, and then packed all our equipment for the trip.

We spent only one day at Patriot Hills, preparing our sleds for the flight to Berkner Island for the start of our journey. Time was of the essence, and we needed every minute we could muster out on the ice skiing. The staff at ALE was a bit amazed that we wanted to fly right away. Typically, extended ski trip groups remain in camp for several days, double- and triple-checking small details or adjusting gear. But we were ready and wanted to fly as soon as the weather permitted.

The following day, November 13, 2009, we were dropped off on Berkner Island with our two overstuffed 320-pound sleds. The pilots wished us good luck and snapped a photo of us mock skiing away, and then the plane disappeared headed back to Patriot Hills. As I looked over my sled that would carry my world for the next seventy-five days, I marveled at everything it contained.

On our first day of skiing across the Berkner Island ice, we covered 11.7 nautical miles. This would be considered a long-distance day on any South Pole ski trip. We had extremely heavy sleds, so this was a positive jump start to the journey. The mileage would begin to decrease as the strain of pulling the heavy sleds set in. We managed to cover pretty good distances across to the edge of Berkner Island, dealing with sore feet and aches daily. Then we entered the sea ice.

Skiing across the Ronne-Filchner Ice Shelf, my emotions were roiling. Underneath my skis, the ocean flowed, separated from me by a layer of solid ice and snow. I kept thinking: What am I doing here? What the hell have I gotten myself into? But at the same time I was awash with excitement and joy, reveling in every moment. These feelings are pretty common at the start of a long and demanding trip when the reality of the endeavor is sinking in. It takes a bit to get into the daily grind that your days will soon become. Each day you go deeper into the adventure, emotions dwindle and you focus on the task at hand. At least that's how I deal with it; others are different, I'm sure.

Throughout the first week of travel, we encountered days of crystal blue skies with warm sun mixed with cloudy, overcast, and chilly days. The sound of the snow crunching under my skis and the weight of the sled I was pulling behind me became my focus. I concentrated on efficiently moving forward, on not wasting any energy. For the next few months, I would subsist on a carefully designed diet that would theo-retically provide me with enough energy to survive. There would be no caches of food awaiting us on the ice. Everything we had was in the sleds, and I needed to make sure I was not burning through calories too fast by flailing away on the snow. Plus, I didn't want to look stupid to my part-ner, who seemed to glide effortlessly forward on her skis—those damn Norwegians. I vowed to toss a football with her when this was all done, just to show her what I did growing up.

Antarctica is the driest continent on earth, averaging just six and a half inches of precipitation a year. We expected very little snow to fall on the main part of the continent, but here on the coast at sea level, the rules were different. We had over a thousand nautical miles to cross on this expedition, so we wanted to get off to a quick start. The last thing we wanted or needed was a whiteout here on the continually changing sea ice. Also, fresh snow is hard to pull a sled across due to higher friction. We soon learned, however, that fate didn't care about what we wanted.

We pressed on each day in constantly changing weather, pushing hard across the ice shelf with a watchful eye on the horizon for the Dufek Massif in the Pensacola Mountains, which would serve as our passage onto the Antarctic continent. Day after day we skied in whiteout condi-tions. It was akin to being inside an eggshell. The sleds were monstrous to pull, and the surface light was totally flat, rendering surface features we were trying to ski over indiscernible. Frustration and our first real mental tests began to surface. I remember trying to decide if this kind of expedi-tion was supposed to be fun, or if it was what Sisyphus felt like pushing that damn stone uphill forever. Of course, it was beautiful out there, and I knew I was fortunate to be in that spot on such an incredible journey, but quite frankly it sucked a lot of the time.

The mental warfare began each morning when each of us had to decide the reason for getting out of the tent. One day we stopped to discuss the option of putting up the tent midday to wait and see if con-ditions would change, but we quickly came to our senses and continued. There is no time to stop and wait for better conditions in polar ski expe-ditions of this length. Making distance is everything. Your world quickly devolves into hour increments and nautical miles covered; nothing else matters. Things can become hopeless rapidly, yet you have to keep pushing on continually. You are stuck inside your head. One night in the tent, Cecilie turned to me and said, "That was the worst day of skiing I have ever had." Those words, coming from someone I looked up to and who had been through so much at both Poles, made me think only one thing as I fell asleep: What have I gotten myself into?

To maximize our potential, we started to ski longer each day. On the sea ice, we developed a skiing system: We would go for forty-five minutes and stop to rest for twelve minutes. That way, we would not burn out. Once we got off the sea ice, we added five minutes to each of our twelve ski legs each day, which added a whole hour, so now we were moving forward for a total of seven hours per day. We put full-length skins on our skis to gain every centimeter of traction possible while pulling our still very heavy sleds. Soon the conditions got much colder and windier, which helped harden the snow and lower the friction that slowed us down. Soon we started making good time—a huge boost mentally. We also started to break the eleven nautical miles in a day barrier, which was a huge mental hurdle. We were popping "vitamin I"—ibuprofen—pretty regularly and another potent anti-inflammatory called Voltaren like candy at night. It helped ease the pain of sore hips from the harness, aching backs and leg muscles, and most painfully, aching feet.

Just two weeks in, the thoughts of luxuries began to creep into our subconscious. All I could think about was the bag of Doritos sitting in my sled that I had brought to celebrate Thanksgiving Day. My mouth would water in anticipation. It motivated me to keep moving forward and keep my eyes on the prize, crossing the continent.

Journal Entry
82 08.619 N
50 45.008 E
11/26/09
Day 14
Skied 16 Miles

Thanksgiving Day. The Dufek Massif is getting closer. Today was calm, with absolutely zero wind all day. We started out in normal ski clothes and our normal outerwear layers, but by the end of the day, we were down to just wool tops, a headband, and wearing no gloves. It was literally hot. We climbed a good bit, and I believe we are camping tonight on the coast of the mainland of the Antarctica continent buried down below the surface of thousands of years of snow and ice. We are finally off the ocean ice! Yahhhooo! Cecilie has nicknamed this place "Costa del Sol," the sun coast. It is incredibly beautiful with infinite white all around, only broken by the lonesome Pensacola Mountains out our tent door. Silent out now, only sun on the tent walls. It's Thanksgiving Day, and I am so far away from home. Our feet are in pain. Cecilie has a terrible blister on her toe but remains cheerful and simply describes it like this: I just have chubby and social feet. All my toes want to be together. This is the simple smiles and the comfort of the tent.

Thanksgiving was a notable turning point. The Dufek Massif looked close enough to touch, just 3.8 nautical miles away from our lovely little campsite. The tent was warm and happy, and we were next to mountains that only a handful of people had ever seen, let alone experienced, touched, and admired. We slept that night perched close to the Davis Valley. This specially protected area holds Floridas Pond, the Western Hemisphere's most southerly freshwater pond. We both were primed mentally and physically to dive deep into the crossing.

We left camp on the morning of November 28, eager to ascend to the polar ice cap at the top of the Pensacola Mountains and finally be on the Antarctic Plateau, where the main part of our journey would take place.

The morning was incredibly beautiful and crisp. Our goal was to move our camp and sleds up a massive rise to stage the next part of the journey. We skied for a couple of hours and, just before the base of the hill, reached a fantastic blue ice patchwork that extended for several hundred meters in all directions. We could not ski across it, so we switched to the crampons we had in our sleds specifically for climbing the hill that lay ahead. The experience of pulling my heavy sled across that luminous ice was exhilarating, as it began to glide with much less effort.

When we reached the base of the 500-foot vertical rise that lay directly above us, it was difficult to imagine pulling our sleds up such a steep slope. It had been difficult enough skiing on flat terrain with them. We decided to go forward using the technique of two people pulling one sled. Clipping both our pulling lines on one sled, we set off with spirit to attack the hill. For the next several hours, we pulled in five-minute increments, then rested in unison on the slope. It was backbreaking work. We did this all the way to the top, where we stopped to relish the achievement, before peering back down the massive slope, barely able to locate the tiny speck that was our other sled waiting at the bottom.

We were working our way back up with the second sled, feeling pretty confident in our abilities, when I suddenly stepped through a crack in the snow. I sank into a crevasse that swallowed me up to my hip, leaving my foot dangling in the dark open space below. I carefully extricated my lower body, and together we continued to the top. It was an eye-opening reminder that danger lurked everywhere in that frozen climate.

We were twenty days in then, and this was a time—which I would experience on other polar ski expeditions—when you begin to change, to sink into your new normal. Suffering was our constant companion. The rigors of pulling the heavy sleds on varying snow conditions were starting to take their toll, both mentally and physically. I was getting used to skiing with huge heel blisters, and a portion of my big toe that was missing a little bit of the edge from the Everest cold injury was constantly rubbing on my inner boot. I also had painful thigh rubbing from the friction there too, which was miserable. But my Norwegian compatriot had planned for this, as it's a standard malady in distance skiing. She had packed silver sulfide to help with rubbing and burns. I was constantly reminded of something my mother would say when I hurt myself growing up: "Rub some dirt on it and get back in the game." Well, I was living that axiom daily. That is the reality of an expedition to ski to the South Pole. The days were a mixture of discovery and enjoyment juxtaposed by extreme discomfort.

We carefully followed our compass bearing all day long to the next waypoint. We would use these predetermined waypoints of latitude and longitude to navigate around significant terrain features or potentially dangerous crevasse fields identified on the map. We skied across the Sallee Snowfield for several days under the watchful eyes of the Forrestal mountain range, which was slowly disappearing in our rearview mirror. The hills around us were covered in a soft pillow of white, forcing us to ski each day in a whiteout. We had a bead on the Neptune Range and the Antarctic Plateau proper.

Still, this place in between left an everlasting mark in my memory. I talked a lot with Cecilie in the tent about my thoughts on isolated places and how hard it is to verbalize their impact. We nicknamed the area the "Lonesome Mountains," influenced by a hint of Edward Abbey, who I was fond of, and thoughts of my grandmother, who grew up on a ranch in Texas. She'd told us stories of riding her horse to the property fence to exchange dolls with Indian girls that she couldn't understand, but they were friends anyway. She used the term "lonesome" a lot, and I told Cecilie how the American Southwest desert reminded me of this, and about Abbey's book *Desert Solitaire* and his love of places like this.

Journal Entry
December 3, 2009
83 32 216 S
052 05 654 W

I wonder what happens here, in this spot when no one is here? The wind blows, the snow moves around, nothing changes too much . . . ever. I often think about that in wild places, but here it seems ampli-fied. There are no animals or plants to change . . . no people. No one has ever stood in this exact spot I am on at this moment. I look at the mountains that are always here by themselves, and years pass . . . they are beautiful but lonesome.

There is beauty on the ice. It is a truly gratifying experience to ski toward the never-ending white horizons of Antarctica. A unique bond forms between teammates on journeys that are particularly difficult physically, emotionally, and environmentally. You share extraordinary highs while facing the drudgery of traveling countless nautical miles. Proper rest and relaxation are reserved for the end of the trip. The focus is on momentum and the end goal. It can be overwhelming at times, and the hardships can become overbearingly heavy on your shoulders. Just getting up in the morning starts to become a hurdle that must be jumped. Finding the motivation to get out of the sleeping bag and fire up the stove to melt snow into water when the wind is howling around the tent takes effort. The thought of stepping out of your little nylon refuge once again for a full day of near-constant aerobic activity and ever-present hunger can be overwhelmingly demoralizing.

Food was one of our most basic needs and became the most wonderful thing in our little world, taking on somewhat magical properties of pleasure and satisfaction. We were skiing for roughly eight to ten hours a day by now, and our bodies had begun to melt away the excess weight put on pre-expedition. I had purposefully gained around eighteen pounds while training for the trip, mostly from eating tons of pasta with liberal use of olive oil as well as finishing virtually every meal with ice cream. I know it may sound like heaven for some, but it felt more like work sometimes. Gaining weight was difficult for me, a phenomenon that is, unfortunately, changing with age. The preloading reminded me of constantly trying to bulk up for football, but it was needed. On the trip, we would be burning around 8,000 calories per day. It was virtually impossible to take in enough calories to offset that, so any extra body fat would be stored energy.

Throughout the entire expedition, I would burn roughly 560,000 calories. When you are consistently in that kind of deficit, even marginally tasty food takes on magical properties. A frozen energy bar midday? Absolutely incredible. Gobbling down a huge handful from our premade "lunch bags" stocked with salty nuts and generous helpings of chocolate? Mind-blowingly unbelievable. Savoring an entire bag of pre-dinner Doritos? Simply heaven. Weight was a more significant concern than space in our massive sleds, so bringing things like chips was surprisingly easy. Plus they were the most fantastic thing in the world at the end of a long day.

Lounging in the tent after a full day of skiing was often very comfortable, especially if there was little wind and the sun was on the tent wall. We would enjoy a pre-dinner snack for extra calories, a rustic appetizer plate. Often it would consist of Wasa bread with salami and olive oil, the latter two items having been thawed next to the stove as we melted water for dinner. The other great thing about the end of the day was we had time to talk. During the day we would only stop for a brief snack, sometimes muttering a few words in passing if someone was having a particularly bad day. The tent was a time to exchange thoughts, ideas, and even future plans. We talked a lot about home, and I learned all kinds of interesting facts from Cecilie. Such as the name of Donald Duck in Norway, Kalle Anka, and that she had never had a hamburger until she was twenty-one years old. That, of course, was particularly mind-blowing to an American. These moments only strengthened my feelings for her.

Over many days, the mountain range behind us disappeared, and we were now in the land of zero visual landmarks, only continuous white with some wind features on the surface in all directions. The sun was high in the sky, and up for twenty-four hours a day in the Antarctic summer. It would circle us each day. We had become tuned in to the angle of our shadows on the surface, sometimes using that as a temporary bearing to follow for short distances in a one-hour block of ski time. Out in the elements for a twenty-four-hour day, we became very in touch with the natural world, discovering small, intricate details we might not otherwise have noticed. Things like the sun rising higher in the sky as the days passed, how the snow surface changed the higher we climbed in elevation, or the amount of sastrugi (snow waves caused by wind) increasing with new degrees of latitude. Subtle changes in the environment had a distinct impact on the snow surface. As we slowly skied toward the center of Antarctica and the South Pole, the difference in prevailing wind direction and altitude wreaked daily havoc on the snow surface, issues we would have to overcome.

As the days passed, we began to look forward to celebrating Christmas. The holiday had become a short-term goal to focus on and would serve as one of only a few half-days of rest during the entire trip. We were hauling an extremely small and light but precious package of letters and surprises from our families to celebrate Christmas in style. I was looking forward to the much-needed rest even more than the food at this point. The anticipation of waking up and skiing for just six hours and then lying in the tent the rest of the day was almost too much to bear. It began to work against my mental state as I yearned for that day to hurry up and arrive. I felt like a grumpy child again—happy one minute, irritated the next. As we came within two weeks of Christmas Day, there seemed to be nothing to look forward to in the near term. There was only constant skiing and too much thinking day in and day out on the same topics as the time slowly passed from ski block to ski block.

Journal Entry
December 10, 2009
Skied 22.8 km
6.5 hours
85 07 960 S 52 38 492 W

This was my worst day so far, or at least the worst ending to a day. We skied with short skins on our skis the first three blocks this morning, and the terrain is hard with big sastrugi, so it became challenging to climb over them without losing grip on the surface since our sleds want to pull us back. So, we switched to long skins for more friction. We skied three more blocks, but now it was way too much friction, and we were going nowhere fast. So, we made the terrible mistake of switching skins yet again to medium size, which would have been perfect. However, we had pulled these on and off so often in the cold the adhesive cannot hold. This was when my issues started with my skin coming off. We stopped and taped the end, hoping for a temporary fix. It worked, but then it acted as a brake on my ski, so I stopped and took off the tape, slowly gaining frustration. Then the skin came all the way off my ski. So, I put a short skin back on and almost made it for an hour before it too came off once again. We stopped, bitched a lot at each other, and put up the damn tent. I feel melancholy like never before on the trip. The skins made me think negative thoughts and get down. When we stopped, I was cooked mentally and did not put up a good enough fight to keep myself going. I am pissed and need to get over it.

By the next day, the pendulum had swung back again, as evidenced by this journal entry: "YAHOOO 30.3 kilometers [16.4 nautical miles] skied today. We came back with a vengeance and kicked ass!"

This mental factor, more than anything, would become a great game. The challenge of remaining mentally positive day in and day out can be the most challenging aspect of a long polar ski expedition. The key to pushing on was that when these swings in mood and attitude would present themselves, you had to be able to make a change inside your head no matter what. If you had a lousy two-hour block of time because you felt sorry for yourself, or if a negative thought from the real world seeped into your mind, then you had better find a good thought to counter it. It became common for an entire day to be either overwhelmingly positive or negative. We relied on each other to lift the mood and show each other how lucky we were to be in this place and moment.

Listening to music helped immensely. Though it was a hassle to set up my earphones underneath all the layers, it paid off in spades to be able to listen to inspiring tunes. I used a mixture of rock, rap, country, and a little bit of everything to keep the variety going.

Regardless of our mental state, the incredible reality was that we were making a considerable amount of progress. The week before Christmas, we reached the 87th degree of latitude, which had become notorious over the years as being home to the largest sastrugi along this route. This was an issue for a few reasons, most importantly because sastrugi slow you down. Paying attention to the snow surface ahead and making minor adjustments in the ski track interrupt the flow of keeping your head down and following a compass bearing. It's a problem when the weather is terrible and the light gets flat, because it becomes much harder to anticipate a three-foot snowdrift in your path if you can't see it until on top of it. Even worse is skiing over and off the backside of these little drifts when you are not even aware you are on one. Suddenly you ski off a bump and almost fall over, again and again, all day long. But the real problem was knowing that we were in the middle of a notorious sixty-mile stretch of them. It got in our head and messed with us mentally. So waking up in the morning to clear, sunny weather became an increasingly joyous occasion, making the day easier, faster, and much more enjoyable.

By now, we were reaching the heart of the route to the South Pole. The prevailing winds consistently came over our left shoulder, hitting us on the side of the face like a brutally cold slap. The ambient temperature was 30 degrees below zero, so when the winds picked up, we would leave the tent wearing all our layers, an extra wool shirt, and a face mask to protect exposed skin. We even donned our down vests for extra core body warmth. The danger in that many layers, however, is because you are essentially doing an aerobic workout in hostile temperatures when skiing and pulling a heavy sled, the moment you stop, it gets cold, and any sweat on your skin becomes a serious threat. The key is to try to maintain a constant equilibrium inside your little clothing-encapsulated world—seemingly subtle acts like unzipping your armpit zippers before you get overheated become second nature.

The biggest challenge in layering often comes on the head and face. Temperatures below 30 degrees coupled with bitter winds can be instantly dangerous to exposed skin, especially on cheeks, nose, and ears, where blood flow is limited. You have to wear a face mask and goggles to avoid the risk of superficial skin damage. The problem is that you cannot wear too much on your head or you risk sweating since you are almost always aerobic. Hence, a delicate dance of layering our heads with a wool hat, balaclava, and neck gaiter ensued. The end result frequently was a sizable frozen icicle forming in front of our mouth on the mask from the moisture in our exhalations. Melting and drying our face masks next to the stove became a routine task each night. I cannot imagine how hard it must have been for earlier explorers in these regions.

As our little holiday on ice approached, we reached another short-term objective by skiing into the 88th degree of south latitude. The sastrugi were beginning to subside, and things were looking up. Each day now, we were covering an average of 14.6 nautical miles, and the South Pole was indeed on the horizon—albeit still 120 nautical miles away.

Journal Entry
Xmas Eve
December 24, 2009
88 19 813S 54 25 475W

A very nice day. We awoke at the normal time of 6 am and out of the tent and on skis at 8 am. We did a half-day of skiing for six blocks and stopped for Christmas. We have been in the tent since 2 pm lounging, eating, and calling home. We drew a Christmas tree on the tent wall and put the cards and presents at the bottom. Complete with silver streamers and a Santa ornament! We are already full of chocolate— opening cards and relaxing. We lay here 100 nautical miles from the South Pole. Warm in the sun-filled tent even though it is -20 outside. Merry Christmas to all at home. I'm a little homesick today . . .

The following days were sluggish and hard, with the hoarfrost on the surface slowing the sleds and our skis. Still, we persisted, drawing ever closer to the midway goal of reaching the South Pole. We hit the usual hurdles of mind, body, and equipment. Like a long sailing voyage, you find yourself constantly regrouping and fixing broken gear, bodies, and spirit. We were now confident that we could use our medium-sized skins on the skis for the remainder of the trip since we had done most of the uphill to the Pole, so we screwed them onto the bottom of our skis. We had a close call when a filling came out of one of Cecilie's teeth, exposing a nerve that could have become a real problem in the cold air. Thankfully we had a dental kit in the first-aid supplies, and I played dentist for part of a day, putting a temporary filling in place. That's something I should put on my résumé! On December 29, we hit a new record with 17.5 nautical miles in a single day, and things quickly turned positive again.

The South Pole was just two days of skiing away, and we could feel the heightened energy in our little team.

On December 30, we covered yet another 16.7 nautical miles, and knew we had to be close to the Pole. On the first pitch of Cecilie's last ski block, I was lost in my own world listening to music on my iPod when suddenly she turned around and yelled to me, "Ryan, look!" Startled out of my world, I looked up, and far on the horizon saw buildings.

Journal Entry
December 31, 2009
12 pm Chilean Time
90 00 000 S
53 00 000 W
South Pole

How do I describe . . . the feelings. As I sit here in the tent, the emotions come on stronger and stronger. At first, I just wanted to get here. It has been extremely cold and windy today. Finally, here we can relax and celebrate the start of a new year. We are warm in the tent, eating chocolate and drinking tea—a huge milestone on this amazing journey. A big new US building is impressive, sitting on the vast snow of forever. A dark grey two-story out-of-place structure on stilts is sitting just adjacent to the South Pole. There are storage containers neatly lining the scientific drilling operation. They are taking down the historic old dome that has sat here for decades. Amazing.

I had mixed emotions the day that we skied away from the South Pole station. Mostly I felt a sense of rejuvenation and excitement for the extraordinary journey that remained in our path. But our little world of isolation had been shattered by the sudden introduction of people, machines, and the muted chaos of everyday life thrust upon us in the middle of the Antarctic ice. We had skied for forty-nine days to reach the South Pole, completely alone, with no outside sounds except the wind.

We did everything independently while camped for one night at the ALE site, which lies a few hundred meters from the South Pole. All offers of help were kindly refused. We were on an unsupported expedition, which meant taking nothing from outside our little bubble. It was hard to say no to a freshly brewed cup of coffee, even more so to a meal from their on-site mess facilities. One of the station's scientists even offered to "mistakenly leave" a care package along our pathway the next day. We politely turned him down. We were committed to our expedition and would not entertain any thoughts of cheating.

We both felt quite eager to depart the South Pole and return to our isolation. We felt a pureness and self-reliance together that was incredibly empowering, and we wanted to get back to our simple routine.

I've often heard adventurers who partake in long, rugged expeditions in harsh conditions reminiscing about the simplicity that life takes on. As the days pass, you strip away the perceived but essentially manufactured connections we all have to everyday luxury items. You begin to slowly settle into a rhythm of natural day-to-day living based on your actual, limited needs.

It was good to have gained so much repetitive experience during the stretch from Berkner Island to the South Pole because the terrain that lay ahead was anything but forgiving. Now, skiing the opposite way from help and the little bit of infrastructure on the ice was both scary and intoxicating.

Things were clicking so well. We could navigate in whiteouts with little difficulty, fix any gear problem that reared its ugly head, and deal with terrible weather if need be. The thought that began to creep into my mind was that as long as we stayed healthy, without any catastrophic accident to either our bodies or a vital piece of equipment, there was no way we would not be successful. Our relationship was humming along, too, which is unusual for long polar ski journeys, where arguments, jealousy, and egos often strain team dynamics. I was entirely in it now. Mentally I had swallowed the polar Kool-Aid and was genuinely committed to seeing this expedition through to the end, no matter what.

The trip to the South Pole had been challenging since the finish line had felt so far away. Each day it was over the horizon, somewhere out of sight. The mental struggles of unzipping a sleeping bag in shitty weather, or pulling on frozen boots, had felt far more significant initially. Now we could see the goal as obtainable, and we were on the downward slope, at least mentally. An exciting vibe infused our small team, and we felt like true hardcore adventurers.

It was perfect to leave the Pole with a positive attitude because our near future involved climbing higher in altitude. We were headed into the most extreme cold and wind of the trip. Each day took us toward an ominous-sounding feature that we would never know we were on without the knowledge of altitude, the Titan Dome.

The SCAR Composite Gazetteer of Antarctica is a composite of scientific names that delineate features of Antarctica taken from aerial photography and echo-sounding projects that mapped the continent over the years. The ominous feature that lay directly in our path was a high, broad snow rise first crossed by the earliest pioneers of Antarctica travel, the Amundsen and Scott expeditions. It would later be named after the Titan computer at Cambridge University, used to process the radio-echo-sounding data that mapped the region.

So, our "it's all downhill from here" mentality still had quite a bit of challenging uphill terrain to conquer. For us, it did not matter. We were excited to ski up and over the Titan Dome and get on with the business of skiing toward the other side of the continent. The wind was blisteringly cold as we slowly skied each day to successively higher altitudes. Unrelenting gusts swept across the surface, creating constant whiteouts for several days in a row. The higher altitude also made the snow surface more resistant to our forward progress, with greater friction.

I found it easier to be in the front position now because it meant I could focus on the compass and navigation work. That was better than being in the back position, where although the skiing was more manageable, you were stuck with only your thoughts for endless hours. We were now skiing upward for nine hours a day, ready to hit the literal top of the hill and start the long journey to the coast. Better weather moved in as the days ticked by, and the whiteouts turned to cold, crisp, sunny days with puffy clouds and incredible blue skies. We were making significant progress and knew that someday we would look back on this time and wish we were here again.

Journal Entry
Day 59
January 10, 2010
87 38 593 S
165 38 115 E

The unique thing about this place, this time, and the journey is that we are in a place that is so hard to reach and many people would yearn to see. The irony is each day, we are working hard in our heads to be somewhere else, dreaming of other places that are really quite easy to reach, like a bed, or a couch, or a beach. This sport lies in stark contrast to something like rock climbing when the sun is shining on your back, and you are totally focused on the exact spot you are in right then and there. Nothing else strays into your head, and you have complete focus in the moment. I remind myself not to constantly search for something else to think about and enjoy this, because I am sure after this trip ends, I will be desperately wishing I was back here in this exact spot. You would not trade that moment in time for the world.

On day fifty-six of our ski journey, we reached an altitude of 10,380 feet. We had made it to the top of the dome. Knowing that now we were heading down toward the sea was an incredible feeling, and we were excited to dive headlong into the next challenge. We knew that getting over the Titan Dome was a massive hurdle in many ways, and we took that positive feeling forward with us. That was important since we still had landmarks with ominous-sounding names like "The Devil's Dance Floor" and "The Butcher" directly in our path.

On January 11, we reached a mental high point that is hard to describe. About three ski blocks into our day, we saw something that filled our spirits with a magical, uplifted feeling. Far away on the horizon were mountains, snowy peaks that interrupted the perfect horizontal line of our usual horizon. They were the Transantarctic Mountains, which marked the edge of the Antarctica mainland. We could distinguish what we believed to be Mount Howe, a peak close to the Beardmore and Liv Glaciers, as a high point on our map. More importantly, somewhere out there was Mount Nansen, which sits adjacent to the Axel Heiberg Glacier. That glacier marked the entry point onto Antarctica for Amundsen's party on the first successful trip to the South Pole. It would serve as our exit point off the mainland down to the Ross Sea. This towering mountain massif was out there, still a ripple on the horizon far away, but it was there! We put up the tent, crawled into our little oasis for the evening, and discovered that we had set a new distance record of twenty-one nautical miles in a day. My shoulder was in constant pain from the repetition of movement, but I didn't care. We had real, tangible landmarks and the momentum of covering vast swaths of distance on our side.

It was somewhere along this part of the trip that I was really feeling the rigors of so many days out on skis. The physical part was difficult, but the mental challenges of skiing for so many hours and days were even more so. I talked with Cecilie several times in the tent about the proposed North Pole trip with Eric. There would only be around a month and a half in between the two monstrous expeditions if I did join the group there. That thought was weighing me down on the trip I was still on. I made the hard decision to send Eric a satellite text message that I had decided to pull out of one of the spots on the North Pole.

Was I giving up what could realistically be my only shot at a North Pole expedition? I didn't know for sure, but I trusted my guts and made the decision. I knew he would be disappointed because it would throw a hitch into the team finances. Luckily, he was also talking to an additional person, and that ended up panning out. They had three team members in the end, and it was not a big issue.

On long expeditions, there comes a time, usually several weeks into the endeavor, when individuals and teams become so in tune with what needs to happen in a day that the efficiency is impressive. It all comes down to repeating the essential tasks to live and move toward the end goal. Of course, a lot depends on how your group structures your daily routine. This is not as simple as it may sound, but with experience comes judgment, and successful decision making soon follows.

I remember one time on our trip, fairly early on, we had just set up the tent and were moving some gear around. By accident, Cecilie cut the fabric of our fly with a ski edge. It was a simple mistake that anyone could make, but out in the middle of Antarctica, that little cut had the potential to be life-threatening and expedition-ending if not addressed. Before the trip, we had spent many hours assembling an extensive repair kit. Since you cannot bring a toolbox, each piece of the kit either had a specific purpose or multiple applications to fix many things. There is always the potential for catastrophic failures that can end an expedition immediately: a broken ski, lost tent, broken sole on a ski boot, or even an irreparable ski binding. What we brought had been carefully chosen to cover all contingencies. We had one spare ski and one extra binding that would work for both of us. We had wire and durable line to sew with if a boot sole came apart.

We couldn't afford to lose our tent, so we laid it out flat on the snow and sewed up the tear with dental floss and then covered that with rip-stop tape and seam sealer glue. We hoped that would hold for the rest of the trip.

These are the lessons that come with being an adventurer. Polar adventurers need to be dialed and determined. You learn how to fix things. Starting with yourself physically, you become well versed at antic-ipating slight nagging injuries and taking care of them. Mentally you must be able to fix your head when negative thoughts appear. You need to develop a mentality akin to the Nike motto of "Just Do It," as you don't have the luxury of opting out when you are miles from civilization. Sur-vival demands momentum, not sitting around feeling sorry for yourself. The self-reliance and craftsmanship you develop are rewarding and spill over into regular life.

Another thought started to creep into our subconscious at this point in the trip. What happens when we get there? Similar to long ocean crossings, where sailors commonly display reluctance to leave the boat once they reach the safety of a harbor, we did not necessarily want this trip to end. Cecilie was more mentally challenged by this thought, given that the end meant a return to things that reminded her of her past life with a husband forever gone. Out here, it was just us and the wind. Freedom and silence surrounded us. We knew our jobs: put up the tent, melt water, cook, sleep, take down the tent, pack the sleds, ski, navigate, and repeat. I think this might be one of the reasons people get hooked on expeditions—a longing for simplicity. Our everyday lives are complex: work, commuting, meals, family commitments, friends, and constant news and social media updates. That's why I am one of those people who struggle with the need to dispatch live information on expeditions. While we both worried a bit about the impending conclusion of our trip, we concentrated on ensuring its success and our safety.

On day sixty-two of the trip, we broke a new record for distance in a day: 22.35 nautical miles. At that speed, we could cover a degree of latitude in less than three days. We had momentum, which was good because the next day we skied straight into the massive crevasse field affectionately known as the "Devil's Dance Floor." We knew it was out there and had tried to avoid the area by staying west of our compass bearing, in effect trying to skirt the outer edge of the cracks in the ice. But despite those efforts, we hit the vast area of huge crevasses that had given pause to Amundsen and worried every other explorer who came near the location.

We absolutely did not want to flirt with this giant field of open and hidden crevasses, so we did the conservative thing and backtracked out of the Devil's Dance Floor. Being cautious, we decided to turn hard to the west and ski about twelve miles away from our destination, which was hard to stomach. Finally, feeling like we could get around the dangerous area, we turned back on our compass bearing and skied another twelve miles to position ourselves well away from the whole section. Too close now for careless mistakes.

As we skied, I had a solemn feeling that I could not shake quickly. We were close to the "Butcher's Shop," the location where, during his historic trip to the South Pole, Roald Amundsen ordered the butchering of twenty-three of his forty-one sled dogs for food for the remaining dogs and men. These were his trusted companions that had worked so hard to bring his team deep into the frozen unknown. He praised them in his journal, and then wrote, "In four days, we have reached the plateau from the coast, come and say that dogs cannot be used here. It has been hard work, but now the dogs were to have the best of rewards—death." We stopped for a moment in the location where the grisly deed happened over four days back in November 1911. It was an eerie spot. I could feel the history there, and it made me sad and took some time to shake off.

We were getting close to the top of the access to the Axel Heiberg Glacier and looking forward to going down the "big drop," which would lead us to our exit off the edge of the Antarctica mainland. But the weather gods did not want us off the plateau just yet. The winds were brutally cold, and the visibility was horrendous, to the point that we had to camp for the night with just 4.3 miles to ski to our target GPS waypoint.

After putting up our tent and crawling in as two beaten-down and tired souls, we ate freeze-dried dinners and crashed into our sleeping bags as the winds died down. Soon the still air gave way to sunshine on the tent. We were getting lower in altitude, and so with the sun came warmth. As if we were of one mind, we both suddenly woke up at midnight, overly hot in the sleeping bags. We made a plan to just get on with it. By 2:15 a.m., we were back on our skis.

Thus began one of my fondest expedition memories ever during my career. On January 19, day sixty-eight of skiing, we worked in unison to descend the "big drop," then continued through the "quiet valley" at the bottom. The navigation was intense, and we studied photos we had stashed in our sleds to make sure we were on the right track. We aimed to reach a spot called the "triangle" at the top of the Axel Heiberg Glacier, where the big crevasses began. We knew we needed to ski down to the "triangle" GPS waypoint and continue farther in. We were following Borge Ousland's advice to "go down this slope as far as you dare, and then turn left."

We navigated unroped down through the countless crevasses, switched on mentally and relying on our mountaineering experience. After seventeen hours on our skis, we had covered 21.7 nautical miles in one continuous push. We were at the bottom of the Axel Heiberg Glacier. In my journal, I simply titled this experience as "the day of all days."

We called from the tent that evening to arrange a location for the ALE plane to pick us up in a couple of days. We located a GPS coordinate that was well out on the Ross Ice Shelf. We wanted to make sure we crossed the entire continent of Antarctica and finished on the sea ice.

We went to sleep knowing we had done something special and unique, something that was rapidly wrapping up.

As we skied the final day, we had mixed emotions. It would feel so good to finally stop moving, but at the same time, it would be hard to end this journey. I took out the video camera and asked Cecilie how she felt, and she simply said, "Why would anybody want to leave this place?" I understood her feelings perfectly because I felt the same way.

We woke up on the final morning in our little tent on a vast expanse of ice stretching in all directions. We skied out, made a line of brightly colored stuff sacks as a sight reference for the pilot, and then patiently waited until the DC-3 prop plane circled above. When the pilot landed, he motored over to the camp and positioned the aircraft with one wing directly over our tent. Now that is service.

It was only the two of us and our sleds, along with ALE partners Peter McDowell and Mike Sharp, in the huge plane for the roughly five-hour flight back to Patriot Hills. A party was waiting for us, complete with a Norwegian and an American flag, and lots of good food and drinks! As we socialized with the ALE staff and celebrated, I will never forget Peter casually mentioning to me, "Hey Ryan, you know we now have a shower here that you are welcome to use?" I said that sounded like a great idea, but just kept on drinking beers and hanging out. After another twenty minutes, Peter sidled up to me again and said, "Ryan, you guys need to go take a shower." Yep, we were back in civilization again.

As we boarded the return flight to Chile, we were elated but still felt that sense of melancholy at knowing such a fantastic journey was over. When the plane took off from the great white continent, I wondered if I would ever return to this stunning place. It had left a mark on me, and there was still an objective there—what would be the last of my Seven Summits, Mount Vinson.

CHAPTER SIX

Sail Away and Show Business

AFTER CECILIE AND I HAD FINISHED THE JOURNEY ACROSS ANTARC-tica and returned to South America, we decided to take a brief mini vacation in Buenos Aires before flying onward. It felt so amazing to meander the streets of Buenos Aires for several days and decompress in the warm sun. We discussed several options of what could come next, both in our personal and professional lives. As we relaxed in the Palermo Soho neighborhood, soaking up the civilization, we decided it made the most sense for her to return home to Norway and for me to head back to the United States.

She had numerous commitments to fulfill back home. There were multiple television appearances and additional speaking opportunities already stacking up for her. The Antarctica crossing was something special, and the Scandinavians knew this. That was in stark contrast to the reaction back home in America. The day the news broke that we had completed a seventy-day unsupported and unassisted crossing of the Antarctica landmass, the media across America was focused on the story of Plaxico Burress. He was the star wide receiver for the New York Giants who had accidentally shot himself in the leg while in a bar. It is interesting to see what is considered sports news in different parts of the world.

Soon I found myself in a position I had become all too accustomed to in my life. I was homeless and back in Boulder rummaging through a pile of dusty duffle bags to find the keys to a storage unit on the edge of town. I had to find a new place to crash short-term since my buddy Doug Sandok's basement, my home before Antarctica, now had another outdoor guide living there. The thought of spending a couple of months bouncing around on people's couches was getting old; I wondered if I should put a few roots down somewhere.

I had landed in the United States to zero fanfare. A few magazines had reached out and I had answered some online questions, but beyond that, no one really cared about what I had accomplished. I found myself falling into a void, which is common for adventurers after a major project. I felt a sense of emptiness without a big expedition to grab my focus. The ease of society, with all of its conveniences, was overwhelming. I longed for the simplicity of being in the wild spaces of the planet.

It didn't help that I missed Cecilie. Our relationship was moving past being just friends, and I felt an emptiness in my life back in Boulder. But I knew she needed time to do her thing back home without having the distraction of me hovering nearby. So I set about doing what I knew best, looking for my next expedition or guiding gig. I knew I needed to keep the momentum going for my career and with Mountain Professionals. My personal life would sort itself out over time.

I started to think hard about finishing the Seven Summits since I was so close. I had ascents of Everest, Kilimanjaro, Denali, and Aconcagua under my belt, so I only had three more to go. I had attempted Mount Elbrus, the highest point in Europe, several years earlier, but bad weather had stymied my attempt at a summit. I knew that I could climb it under the right conditions. That peak, along with Mount Vinson in Antarctica and Carstensz Pyramid in Indonesia, were all that was left on my list. While I thought about the Seven Summits, I also started thinking about going to the North Pole to complete the True Adventurers Grand Slam. A genuine North Pole expedition was a significant undertaking, one that I had no means of doing right then. Still, I vowed to keep my ears open for a chance if one presented itself one day.

Before the Antarctica expedition, Dave and I had discussed via emails what direction to take the guiding company. We were both bouncing around the world on personal trips and the odd guiding work we put together with clients. Though we were creating the basis of an actual company, it was floundering as we both circled the world on our own paths. In 2008 we had taken a few concrete steps to establish Mountain Professionals. We had made an official office in Boulder, put together documents and policies, invested in higher-quality insurance, and built a new website.

We recognized that the scattered approach to running a business was not a sustainable way for two people to make a living. I had initially told Dave before I left for Antarctica that he could take over the company full time if he wanted because, in my mind, I saw so much potential for a partnership with Cecilie. The European market was rife with possibilities for the two of us if we teamed up—opportunities to put together guiding trips, sponsored expeditions, and even television shows for the Norwegian or European markets.

But Dave was trying to figure out if owning a guide service was the direction he wanted to take in his own life, and he was stalling on committing as much as I was. He eventually decided to go back to school for a master's degree. I saw the writing on the wall and knew what needed to happen. So, before the Antarctica trip, I bought him out of ownership. I was now the 100 percent owner of Mountain Professionals. Upon returning to the United States, I decided to make the company my main gig and pour all my energy into developing the guide service.

I managed to find a one-bedroom basement apartment for rent on a month-to-month basis in downtown Boulder and embarked on a personal mission to make Mountain Professionals grow. I decided to go on all of our trips as the lead guide and audit the entire program in each location. I was also working hard to convince potential clients to go to the remaining Seven Summits on my personal tick list. This would allow me to pursue those mountains and establish them as expeditions for the company.

In the summer of 2010, Cecilie and I eventually agreed that I should, for lack of a better term, move to Norway. I was elated that she felt like taking our relationship a step further, and the idea of moving to Oslo was quite exciting. She was going to be on the Norwegian version of *Dancing with the Stars*, which would take place that autumn. To make things more interesting for the viewers, she arranged to guide a trip to Kilimanjaro in

August, and her dance partner on the show, Tobias, would also go on the trip. Besides Tobias, she had a list of other clients signed up for the trip, and she asked me to come along as another guide.

I made plans to move to Oslo, packing everything I could think of into about five duffle bags to uproot and head across the pond. Most of it was mountaineering gear because, as Cecilie put it, "We can just buy you new clothes over here." Maybe my fashion sense was a little too mountain dirtbag chic at the time.

I boarded a flight bound for Oslo, having said a soft goodbye to Boulder. All I needed to run my guide business remotely was my computer and Melissa Beckwith, my part-time administrative employee. She lived in Colorado and could handle the mail and banking. I was going full bore into a new country, a new relationship, and a new adventure.

It was an exciting time when I landed in Norway. Cecilie had bought a renovated apartment in an up-and-coming area of Oslo. The two-bedroom flat had a couch, a master bed in one of the bedrooms, plates to eat off, and little else. I had a roof over my head, but more importantly, it felt immensely grown up to be living with a girl. But I wasn't there long; within days of my arrival to Norway, I was off to Mount Elbrus in Russia with a group of clients for a Mountain Professionals trip.

One of the more memorable experiences of my life occurred during this trip. The expedition itself was pretty uneventful and straightforward. Along with seven clients, I made quick work of the mountain and reached the summit quickly. I had ticked off another of my goals and was as delighted as my clients. We were in celebration mode while flying back to Moscow from the Caucasus region and ready for a final night on the town.

That plan was derailed on the tarmac when we landed in Moscow. After a short taxi toward the gate, the enormous Cold War–era Russian airliner came to a sudden halt. After about thirty minutes of standing still, the engines shut off, and we sat there with nothing happening. It was the hottest summer on record in Moscow. The plane's interior quickly heated up since there was no air circulation. Sitting in the back rows were the only foreigners on the entire plane, aside from a couple of Chinese travelers who spoke no English, so we had no idea what was happening. After some time, we noticed police cars forming a large circle around the plane. As Russian-speaking flight attendants ran up and down the aisles with no information, we could see a minor scuffle or disturbance down the aisle at the front of the plane. We were mystified.

After about an hour, we noticed there were several military vehicles and, remarkably, many television trucks on the tarmac. I called Cecilie in Norway to let her know something was very wrong on this plane. Within a minute of hanging up, a reporter from *V.G.*, the largest newspaper in Norway, called to ask me what was happening! I told him I had no idea. Desperate, I called the US embassy in Moscow to alert them to our situation. The desk officer told me to wait a moment while he checked the cables. "We have a report that there is a hijacking currently happening at the Moscow Airport tarmac," was his response. My reply, "Yep, we are on that plane!"

He informed me there was nothing they could do, but they would be monitoring the situation. Not much help, I thought. After about two hours in the sweltering heat, the situation onboard was worsening. With no air conditioning, it felt like we were in an oven; men were taking off their shirts, and people were getting delirious. We managed to decipher through broken English from a flight attendant that the hijacker was holding a crew member hostage with some weapon.

Although it was tense and we had no idea what to do, my group remained remarkably calm. Things began to get dire inside that tube. The negotiators finally convinced the perpetrator to allow a doctor on board. People were literally passing out from the heat. The doctor turned out to be Russian Special Forces in plainclothes, and the result was not good for the hijacker. After a scuffle at the front of the plane, we watched through the window as the military roughly escorted a battered and bloody Georgian separatist down the jetway stairs and essentially throw him in the back of a waiting van. The whole incident revolved around this man's idea that he would hold someone hostage with a weapon until Vladimir Putin agreed to meet with him. It didn't work.

It was one of the craziest scenes I can remember, and we were in shock but elated that we would finally be taxied to the gate and get the hell into our hotel late that night. But the actual hijacking was just the beginning of our ordeal. Instead of being set free, as we naively thought, we were led under the airport to a stark holding room. There the police began interviewing every one of the 200 or so people on the plane, individually for some reason. Guess who was the last group? The foreigners. We waited rather impatiently for almost eight hours, through the night. Toward morning, we were desperate and started calling every person we knew of any importance back home for help. We talked to members of Congress, government officials, and anyone else we thought might have some clout. At some point, I think my dad even spoke with the FBI.

With a helpless feeling and a marginally qualified English interpreter who finally showed up near the bitter end of the ordeal, it was our turn to go through an interrogation of over fifty questions. It was brutal. Our group was now in danger of missing our morning flights out of Russia, and we tried to convey this to the authorities. It came to a head when one of my American clients, Al, a Vietnam veteran from another era of thinking in US/Russian relations, was called forward. He had had enough of the short and snarky police captain who knew a little English. After the Russian insulted Al, something inside of Al snapped. He spat on the floor near the petty tyrant in an ill-fitting police uniform and yelled, "You can't hold my friends here anymore!"

Thankfully, someone with a cooler head and some authority saw that things were getting out of hand. They quickly escorted the remainder of my group out the door and into the main terminal of the Moscow airport. There they freed us to get on our way before the whole thing erupted in a replay of Cold War–style confrontation. I checked Mount Elbrus off the Seven Summits list with a remarkable ending.

I spent a few weeks in Oslo before the Kilimanjaro trip in August. It was amazing to get to know the Norwegian summer, most of which was spent in climbing gyms or at rock climbing crags around the city. Other times we traveled around to meet Cecilie's family and friends and to address my city clothes situation in some costly shops downtown. It was during this time that we realized both of us had an interest in sailing.

I had always dreamed of someday trying to sail around the world after reading a book called *Maiden Voyage*, which profoundly impacted me. Tania Aebi told her own story as a privileged young woman floundering in a life of excess and self-described failures. Nothing was succeeding for her in school or in figuring out what direction to take in her life. After watching his daughter struggle, her father gave her two choices. She could enter college, or he would buy her a sailboat. The catch with the sailboat was that she would need to sail around the world. At eighteen years old, she chose the sailboat option. Her story is fantastic. The adventures and hardships she encountered and overcame were mind-blowing. The challenge of such a prospect was eye-opening when I was a youth. The thought of that kind of freedom to adventure was intoxicating. I always kept the idea as a secret personal goal for someday in my future. So when Cecilie mentioned to me that she had always wanted to get a sailboat, that memory resurfaced. We discussed it and decided to pursue it later, but a seed had been planted, one that would bloom in the future.

The time finally came for us to leave for Tanzania. The group probably numbered ten clients plus Tobias and a videographer. Understandably, they were focused on promo shots and short videos that the production company likely told them to capture for the show. I mainly was guiding the group on the climb. The tension was almost immediate, nothing terrible but mildly uncomfortable. Though Cecilie and I were a couple at this point behind the scenes, it was not formal or known in public, which created a weird dynamic.

Regardless, the Kilimanjaro climb went quite well, and from there I flew off to lead the clients on a safari in the Serengeti. I was drinking cold beers and gin and tonics while Cecilie and Tobias returned to Oslo to start rehearsals for the show. From the Kilimanjaro trip all the way through the return to Oslo, the dance pair had spent all their waking hours together, which was hard for me to process. I knew Tobias was gay, but it almost didn't matter. The amount of time they needed to work together was crazy, and they were forming this very intimate working relationship that would make anyone jealous.

When I returned to Oslo to a bare-bones apartment and a secret girlfriend that I only saw in passing, reality began to creep in. Though it appeared cool to be dating a celebrity, it wasn't that great most of the time. I basically sat in an empty apartment for weeks while the TV show went on and on and she was out in the public eye. I went to one of the show tapings, and while I was backstage, I was photographed by the Norwegian equivalent of *People Magazine* in a paparazzi photo. The caption said something equivalent to "who is this tall American that is always around Cecilie." She still had not publicly announced our relationship, and I grew tired of sitting around an empty apartment.

In hindsight, I should have taken off for some personal travel throughout Europe. I could feel a deep jealousy building due to the pressures of the TV show and the time Cecilie spent with Tobias. We agreed that I should go back to Colorado for a while until the whole TV show adventure was finally over.

It was probably a good thing to do. I had managed to arrange a Mountain Professionals trip to climb Carstensz Pyramid in Indonesia with two clients. I was stoked to focus on that climb and the opportunity to run a company trip while knocking off another of the Seven Summits. I concentrated on that and let the chaotic buzz surrounding me in Norway die off.

The highest summit of Australia is a mountain called Kosciuszko. At 7,310 feet tall, with a road most of the way to the top, Kosciuszko is not a challenge to climb. You can just walk up. So, after some dissuasion among mountaineers throughout the years, it was informally decided that the whole Oceania region would be used to define the tallest mountain for that part of the world. Carstensz Pyramid, or Puncak Jaya as it is locally known, became the climber's summit for that region. With an elevation of 16,024 feet, it is a much more challenging piece of rock to climb.

Located in a remote part of western Papua, Indonesia, Carstensz Pyramid is a massive fin of limestone that requires technical skills to climb and is oozing with adventure. Things have always been complicated getting to the mountain, which is pretty remote. I found a local agent in Papua, New Guinea, to be Mountain Professional's logistical partner. Soon I was winging my way there, ready to tick another summit off my list. But there would be some drama.

One of my clients was a Norwegian named Bjorn, and he needed to leave from Oslo, but a volcano was erupting in Iceland, wreaking havoc on air travel for all of Europe. My other client, Paul Adams, and I were leaving from the United States and flying west, so it didn't affect our journey. I thought, "Great, I finally got a Carstensz trip together, and 50 percent of the clients are not going to be able to go on the trip because of volcanic ash in the air half a world away." I had barely managed to piece these two guys together to make the trip happen and had even fronted part of the money to pay for the helicopter to get there. I had no idea how I would make it work or if I would lose most of the money already sent to Indonesia if Bjorn couldn't get there. In the end, he managed to fly out of Europe just in time and was on his way to meet us in Jakarta.

While on my flight from Tokyo to Jakarta, Mount Merapi in Indonesia erupted, spewing yet another obstacle of ash into the air on the other side of the world from Iceland. Mid-flight from Japan to Indonesia, my flight was diverted to Singapore. All I could think was, "You have to be kidding me."

After an anxious night in a hotel in Singapore, the airline notified us they could fly onward. We all finally arrived in Jakarta and went about our business of getting to Papua. I remember meeting the New Zealand helicopter pilot in a dark hangar somewhere in Timika. It almost felt like we were arranging a drug deal to get flown into Carstensz Pyramid base camp. There are two options for getting into the base camp. One involves an arduous and adventurous five-day trek through the jungle of Lorentz National Park. In those days, it was not the trek so much that was dangerous, but the myriad of unknowns surrounding the fact that you had to walk through the Dani tribe's land.

Situated almost comically adjacent to the Seventh Summit of Australasia is the Freeport company's Grasberg gold mine. It's the largest gold mine globally and has been the source of years of tension between a US-based company, the Dani tribe, and the Indonesian government. There are years of stories of people trying to walk into the base camp only to be held up along the way, sometimes at gunpoint, by locals demanding money or worse.

The second option for getting to the base camp is to hire a helicopter to fly you in. It's a thrilling ride that almost touches the gigantic limestone spires that make up the range. Nowadays, it is a much more established logistical operation, with several companies safely running the helicopter flights. However, back in 2010, it was still shrouded in some mystery, as your local logistics partner would arrange the flight. The helicopter rides had a feeling of sketchiness back then, like the pilot was just one step ahead of the law. The flight was terrifyingly exciting.

We were dropped at the base of the huge fin of rock with a couple of assistant guides. We made short work of the incredible climb to the summit of the highest peak in the Oceania region. I had managed to nab the sixth of my Seven Summits, again by guiding clients. It was an exhilarating feeling to have not only climbed the mountain myself but also pulled off the commercial trip. In reality the trip was operated at a loss, with me fronting several thousand of my own dollars to make it happen. But I was more than willing to expend my own capital because I saw it as an investment in my business and myself.

After the Carstensz trip, things cooled off with the whole "Dancing with the Stars" drama back in Oslo. Cecilie had unfortunately been voted off the competition. I saw firsthand the feelings that this created in the competitors. Watching vote counts roll in and being "kicked off the competition" by her countrymen must have been hard to deal with mentally. But she took it in stride, even though I knew she was hurting a bit inside. I told her, "You're an adventurer, a badass climber and skier, so who gives a shit what judges and the general public think about how you shake it anyway?"

We spent some good times together in Norway over many months, but still cracks appeared. We both wanted a relationship, but she struggled with balancing that and the many opportunities she was being offered to make speeches and appearances. After the TV show, her popularity in Norway went through the roof. Everywhere we went, people looked at her. It was a strange feeling. I kept thinking that this must be the same feeling you would get being in a relationship with a famous actor in the United States.

I was basically acting as an anchor to Cecilie's career in many ways. I was languishing in Oslo, trying to make my own successful career. I wanted to keep climbing 8,000-meter mountains. That was counter to the direction she was going. She had done so much already. She was the first (and still only female) to complete the True Adventurers Grand

Slam, had climbed several 8,000-meter peaks, including K2, and had all kinds of options for sponsorships and speeches. She even seemed to have a never-ending supply of clients lining up for guided trips with her. These were all the things I was trying to accomplish, yet there I was in Norway, a kept man, supporting all her avenues. In hindsight, it could have been a fun and easy existence, but I am not built that way. I dreamed of running off to Pakistan or pulling every string possible to get clients of my own.

We began to face challenges in our daily life because of these tensions. It was a slow burn, but after some weeks we decided to take a break from the budding relationship even though we loved each other. I missed the United States and Colorado and my friends there. So once again, I flew back to a reset in Boulder. I still wanted to be with her, but it seemed the right thing to do at the moment.

Right away, I missed her greatly and regretted leaving. I grew despondent and tried to reach out, but she still needed space. So I focused on the thing I found myself running to each time I needed to take my mind off my personal life: I planned to go climbing 8,000-meter peaks.

When you spend a lot of time in the Himalayas, you make friends and meet other like-minded climbers. In the search to climb skyscraping summits, it is a good idea to have a deep contacts list of other strong alpinists that you believe may have similar tactics and styles to potentially partner with for a trip.

I made a plan to go back to Nepal in the spring of 2011. My target was the fourth-highest mountain in the world, Lhotse, at 27,940 feet. Located adjacent to Everest, it shares most of the same climbing route, with a high camp detour at the top of the Lhotse Face. So I was familiar with the route at least to high camp after climbing the Nepal side of Everest in 2008. It would be a quasi-guiding trip since I would go with the French climber Sophie Denis, who was paying for services that my company would provide. But she was already an experienced 8,000-meter climber and didn't need much in the way of guiding. I was mostly in charge of the logistics side of things.

Since I was trying to tick off more 8,000-meter peaks, I planned another trip to Pakistan right after Lhotse finished. I had met a Swiss climber named Joelle Brupbacher while in Pakistan back in 2006, and I knew she was gunning to climb several more 8,000-meter mountains. She had already climbed four of the fourteen. We had many conversations about trying to climb Nanga Parbat in the summer of 2011. She would climb Makalu in Nepal during the spring while I was on Lhotse. We would link up after and fly to Pakistan for Nanga Parbat, already acclimatized.

Upon landing in Kathmandu, I met up with Sophie, and we made the general plan for the Lhotse trip with my Sherpa team. Trekking into the Khumbu Valley was pretty therapeutic regarding my estranged relationship with Cecilie. I thought about her all the time, but at least I could focus on a big climb and try to take my mind off my situation as much as possible.

On that trip, my company's logistics partner in Nepal, Tshering Sherpa, asked if we could support an additional team at our base camp for the spring. When I heard about the proposed project, I said sure right away. Two Nepalis—Sano Babu Sunuwar and Lakpa Tsheri Sherpa—were going to attempt an incredible first. Their idea was to try to climb Everest and then fly off the summit using a tandem paraglider back to the base of the mountain or beyond. The catch was, Sano Babu didn't have any climbing experience but was a top-notch paragliding instructor, and Lakpa Tsheri was a climbing Sherpa on Everest, but his initial attempts at paragliding had landed him in a tree on a hill near his hometown of Lukla.

Sharing base camp with these two and their support crew, I was inspired by their ingenuity and sheer guts to try to pull off such a poorly funded and haphazardly planned expedition. They threw caution to the wind, determined to make it happen. I was equally amazed to hear that flying off the top of Everest was just the beginning of their plan. The "culmination" of the idea was to then paddle rivers some 400 miles to the Bay of Bengal on the coast of India. Though Sano Babu was an accomplished paddler, Lakpa Tsheri didn't know how to swim or paddle. On paper, their plan was a no-go from the get-go.

We all had a wonderful time climbing our respective mountains that season. I will never forget how we shared camps and worked together to assist one another. One day in particular stands out, when the two asked me to help them figure out if their paraglider rig would make it over the Nuptse Ridge after taking off from the summit of Everest. The summit, at 29,029 feet, is about the highest place you can take off from anywhere. Still, they needed to clear the towering Nuptse Ridge at its lowest point, around 24,600 feet in elevation.

Using my trusted map skills honed on many instructor trips, from the North Carolina hills to the Patagonia mountains, we pulled out the topographic map of the region. We made a rough calculation, literally on a napkin. They, of course, knew the glide ratio of the specific wing they would use, so we just needed to determine the distance between the two points and the difference in altitude to see if they could clear the obstacle. Feeling just a bit of pressure at the time, I said, "At least it seems like it should work." Their reaction, as it was for all the monumental tasks in front of them, was simply, "Cool, well, let's see if it works."

Sophie, Lakpa Dorjee Sherpa, and I reached the summit of Lhotse on May 19 that year. It was my fourth different 8,000-meter mountain summit. We descended to Camp Two on May 20 and waited anxiously to hear about the progress of Sano and Lakpa on their climb of Everest as they ascended to Camp Four that day. During the early morning of May 21, we were just about to descend over the top of the Khumbu Icefall below Camp One when the radios crackled alive. We looked skyward and watched as the boys floated through the sky on the paraglider, pausing to make small circles, presumably to gain some lift. Then they successfully disappeared over the Nuptse Ridge. We knew they were now flying farther down the valley, and I felt pure joy for them. "Those crazy guys did it," I thought.

After a day packing up base camp, we started the trek out of the valley. We spent the night in Namche Bazaar and attended the Irish Pub's grand opening there, which is still in operation, as the only foreigners. On the following day, during the trek out, we met Sano and Lakpa. They were casually drinking beers at a teahouse patio and sheepishly hiding from the authorities, as there were some questions about the validity of their permits. It was no use, though, word had spread through the valley about their adventure, and everyone wanted to say hello. On the way to Lukla, we stopped at one of our Sherpas' homes and threw a party for the guys.

After many, many beers we decided it was time to do the final forty-minute stretch of the trek into Lukla. It is one of my favorite memories in the Himalayas. We were walking along just at sunset, children tagging along and riding on the shoulders of our group. We were surrounded by joy. Everyone wanted to congratulate Sano Babu and Lakpa Tsheri for pulling off the third ever paragliding descent from the summit of Everest, and for being the first Nepalis to do so.

The pair completed their epic quest to paddle the length of Nepal and India to the Bay of Bengal. Along the way, they braved the river's challenges, navigated down the Ganges through an area of bandits, were robbed at knifepoint, and lived off the food they could scavenge from fruit trees along the way. They reached the Bay of Bengal on June 27, 2011, becoming the first people to descend from the summit of Everest to the Indian Ocean—a literal summit-to-sea voyage on a shoestring budget, based purely on determination. The expedition would gain notoriety from outdoor news outlets over time. With much deserved praise, they won the National Geographic Adventurers of the Year award.

That spring would be tempered by the sad news that Joelle Brupbacher had died on the descent from the summit of Makalu in Camp Three on May 22 after reaching the summit. Clearly, I was not going to Nanga Parbat that summer, and for years after I would happen across our many Skype chats, still in the queue on my computer screen, while making climbing plans. It was becoming all too common to lose friends to the mountains.

When I landed at the airport in Denver from Kathmandu, Eric Larsen called me. He was determined to party on a Sunday afternoon. I reminded him that I had just flown for about two days without much sleep. Still, he insisted, "Get back here to Boulder, there is this 5K run where you drink beers instead of water at rest stops, oh, and you have to wear a costume during the event." What the hell? I rummaged through my bags on the bus back to Boulder to find some semblance of a "costume" and showed up for a cold PBR. Still in my mid-thirties, it was easy to rally and keep burning the candle at all ends!

It was good to be back with friends in Boulder, and we proceeded to party pretty hard that night. I faintly remember gin and tonics and some ill-fated attempts to talk to girls. Eric still reminds me of that night and how I just kind of "fell over at one point" but never used my arms to catch the fall. He is always good at jabs from the past.

I spent that time in Boulder recuperating and licking my wounds, trying to make some sense of where I was in my life. I was happy to be back home, but I also was confused and didn't quite know what to do next. So I looked back to the sky and decided it was time to see if I could close out my Seven Summits passport. I knew I needed to head back to Antarctica.

When I was a beginner mountaineer scraping together money to fly to Mexico or the Andes of South America, somehow piecing together trips to places like Everest and Antarctica against overwhelming odds had seemed like a pipe dream. Now that I was entrenched in the adventure world, things were possible, and it only took some grit to make them happen. I needed to climb Mount Vinson. Having skied across the white continent for seventy days, this didn't seem like such a tall task anymore, merely a financial hurdle to overcome.

I took the route of guiding the mountain, as I had on the other Seven Summits. I knew I could somehow piece together a small band of clients, and I began talking to some contacts from past trips who I figured were also interested in going there to complete their own personal Seven Summits projects. I also needed to establish Mountain Professionals as an approved guide service with ALE to begin operating trips to climb Mount Vinson with clients. Luckily, I had a good relationship with the partners at ALE after completing the ski trip there. It was not a big ordeal to set up our relationship to guide in Antarctica. Mountain Professionals gained the moniker of approved guide service on Mount Vinson; now all I had to do was find some clients, which would take some time.

For the autumn of 2011, I managed to arrange a Mountain Professionals trip with two clients to climb Nepal's Mount Manaslu, 26,781 feet in elevation and the eighth-highest mountain in the world. I was psyched because it was another opportunity to climb and expand my business to another mountain in Nepal. By this time, I had reached the summit of four different 8,000-meter mountains: Everest, Cho Oyu, Broad Peak, and Lhotse. I had attempted but not gained the summits of

K2 and Gasherbrum 2, so adding a classic summit like Manaslu would expand my list of climbs.

I had not talked with Cecilie in many months and figured it was a lost cause. I couldn't believe deep down inside that our relationship was over, but there was nothing I could do. I had to let her decide if that would change. She had planned a summer expedition to the North Pole from Canada with the Norwegian polar adventurer Rune Gjeldnes. I knew Rune from Norway and his completely insane polar résumé of crossing the Arctic Ocean, Greenland, and Antarctica. The pair had to call off the expedition midway due to incredibly challenging environmental conditions, warm weather, and too much open water.

In July 2011, a Norwegian named Anders Breivik detonated a bomb in the center of Oslo, killing eight people. He then took a boat to the island of Utøya and murdered sixty-nine young people at a summer camp with heavy weapons. I could not believe the news when I heard it over the radio as I drove through Boulder. I was thrust back into worrying about people I knew in Norway. I sent a message to Cecilie simply asking if she was okay. Later that day, she responded briefly; at least I knew she was fine.

While I was training and preparing to travel back to Nepal in the autumn of 2011 for Manaslu, I also started researching sailing lessons. I don't know if it was some subconscious desire to pursue a new passion or an intuition of what happened next.

After an entire spring and summer of no communication with Cecilie, other than her brief response to my text about the Oslo bombing, she suddenly called me one day. It was so good to speak to her and hear how things had been going in her life. We had been apart for many months, each of us living our own lives and traveling on our own respective trips and paths. But throughout that time, I always had this deep-seated feeling that our relationship was not over. I could feel that maybe she was rethinking our relationship, too, as we caught up over several conversations the next few days.

Casually one day, she mentioned that she had purchased a sailboat. I was blown away by the details. Apparently, she had been talking with many friends who sailed to inquire about a special kind of sailboat that could travel the world, polar environments included. She had then ordered an aluminum-hulled, forty-five-foot boat from a French boutique manufacturer called Alubat. They make an outstanding and highly sought-after retractable keel boat called the Ovni 45. The aluminum hull allows you to sail in not only tropical waters but also icy polar environments. The retractable keel means the ship has a shallow draft for hard-to-reach places, and you can even use the tides to beach the boat on dry sand.

It would take many months for the factory to build her specific boat by hand in France. It was strange and ironic how this news coincided with my research into sailing lessons.

Within a week, I decided to sign up for sailing lessons somewhere. I had that old feeling of just diving into something, screw the consequences. About two weeks later, I was on a plane to the British Virgin Islands for a weeklong bareboat skipper course. I lived on a fifty-foot Jeanneau sailboat with the captain and three other students, guys from North Carolina in their mid-twenties who were quite hilarious. The experience was so refreshing and exciting. I was hooked. It was exhilarating to be focused on something other than mountains or polar landscapes.

Anytime you get to hang out in the turquoise-blue ocean of the British Virgin Islands is fantastic. But living on a boat, plotting a course to another island, taking the helm, and the thousands of little skills I learned made it unforgettable. On the last evening, our captain suggested a cove that would leave us with a short sail into the marina the following day for the culmination of the course.

Having passed our written exams, things were loose and beers were flowing as we grilled burgers off the stern of the boat. We were making a halfhearted plan to take the dingy over to a famous hole-in-the-wall bar located in the middle of the bay—a floating bar called Willy T's—when around the corner sailed a giant catamaran, the grandest I have ever seen. There must have been thirty people partying hard to loud music on her deck, and several support boats were cruising behind. That was when the captain mentioned, "I wonder if that is Branson; Necker Island is just around that bend, and his son's birthday is this time of year. I partied with them the year before at around the same time in the same bar."

We pulled out the binoculars, and sure enough, it was the *Necker Bell*, Richard Branson's boat, and they were headed for Willy T's to party. We had to rally and make the scene. It was, in fact, a birthday party for his son, who was in his mid- to late twenties, and there was no shortage of young high society British letting loose at the bar. Several quite beautiful girls, younger than me, were flitting about, so I had to try to at least talk to one of them. I proceeded to use the worst introduction line ever as I stood in front of a beautiful, presumably wealthy twenty-five-year-old young lady. The only thing I could think to mutter was "So . . . you're British."

One of my fellow students has never let me live that one down. He sends me text messages with the magnificent phrase, just to laugh at me from time to time. Toward nightfall, I sidled up next to Richard Branson at the end of the bar. As you can imagine, there was no shortage of people trying to talk with him, but he was just sitting there with no shirt on, drinking cocktails and super relaxed. I offered a toast with my beer, did some name-dropping of mutual people we knew in the adventure world, and gave another cheers, and then we promptly jumped off the rooftop deck into the sea. It was a hell of a night.

When I returned to Colorado, I was refreshed and excited for the autumn trip to Nepal. I had to explain to my friends in Boulder where I had vanished for a week. It didn't seem like a big deal to me. Everyone was literally all over the place on trips and guiding at the time. My disappearing overnight seemed perfectly normal to me, but they had been worried. Even now, if I've been missing or out of contact for a while, Eric Larsen will text, "Been on a sailing lesson?"

When August rolled around, I was set to go for Manaslu with my two clients. It was then that I talked to Cecilie once again. She brought up the idea of coming on the Manaslu expedition. I was secretly elated. Because it was so close to the trip, I had to quickly get her on our permit. She had some commitments during the first part of the trip, so we arranged for her to fly to Sama Goan, the village at the base of the mountain, to meet us.

As we made the long and rainy trek into the Manaslu base camp, I was psyched. Not only was I leading a trip to a mountain that I wanted to climb, but Cecilie would soon be flying in to join our team. We had made one rotation up to Camp One to acclimate before she was due to arrive. On a rest day, I trekked down to Sama Goan to meet her helicopter.

The trip proved to be a reunion of sorts for us. We had not formally talked about getting back together, but it was clear we would be from the moment we met again. We had an excellent expedition: It was a good weather year, and we got to hang out with Russell Brice and other colleagues on the mountain. We reached the summit of Manaslu on October 4; I had climbed my fifth different 8,000-meter mountain.

Now that there was some time since our breakup, we agreed we wanted to give the relationship a full go. I went back to Norway with Cecilie after the Nepal trip; Colorado became my storage spot again. She had spent almost a year living in Oslo and had made a cozy home in the apartment, so it didn't feel like a transient spot. This time the relationship was out in the open; she was more comfortable telling people outside her small circle of friends and family. Then she was featured in a big spread in a national magazine article in which she declared she had a new boyfriend. It was liberating just to finally be open about being a couple.

I managed to put together a little group for the first Mountain Professionals Vinson trip, scheduled in December 2011. It was just two climbers, Scott Kress and Ron Sanga, from my 2008 Everest trip, who were just like me, only needing Vinson on their own Seven Summits quest. I did the same thing as on Carstensz Pyramid, in that I coerced the guys onto the trip for an exceptional price and then spent a bit of my own money to guide the trip. I was determined to make it happen in any way possible.

The trip went off flawlessly, except for some ski boot issues that led to blisters and kept us from skiing back down to Union Glacier Camp. Soon the three of us were standing on the summit of Mount Vinson at 16,066 feet. I remember thinking at the time how unlikely the odds were that an ex-football player, fraternity guy, geologist, and dirtbag climbing instructor had reached the highest point on all the seven continents. It had taken a little longer than a decade filled with patience, focus, and more than a bit of luck to pull it off. I, along with the other two, had joined an exclusive club.

Since we had knocked out the climb so quickly, we had some extra time on our schedule. So we did what all adventurers do when suddenly faced with free time in one of the most remote places on the planet—we went looking for fun. ALE allowed us to ski off into the horizon from Union Glacier and climb unclimbed mountains in the nearby range. It was pretty damn cool—a grand celebration for the three of us who had completed the Seven Summits.

Cecilie and I spent that winter doing everyday things. We took trips to climb in France, went skiing around Norway, and generally had a more typical lifestyle. I was content with the new life of normalcy, which to most people would seem adventurous. But I still had the itch to go for more 8,000-meter peaks, and I felt like Cecilie was mostly beyond her dark days with regard to climbing high and sometimes dangerous routes. Since the K2 disaster was now over three years ago, I gently proposed a trip together. I was keen to try to climb the seventh-highest mountain in the world, Dhaulagiri, at 26,795 feet. Somewhat surprisingly, Cecilie said she was interested in going with me that spring.

Even though she had suffered a terrible loss on K2, she was, after all, an adventurer who still had big mountains in her blood and also had a desire to continue to accomplish new goals. She actually one-upped me and proposed an additional idea. After climbing Dhaulagiri, she thought we should then fly to the Khumbu in Nepal. There she would attempt to climb Everest and Lhotse without oxygen. For me, this was a sign that she was back. I took the idea and ran with it.

We planned to go as a two-person team to climb Dhaulagiri that spring of 2012 and set about on a training regime. For the second part of the trip, Cecilie wanted Russell Brice to do the logistics for us on the Everest/Lhotse climb. My team would handle our first climb. Since we would already be acclimatized, we would fly directly to Everest Base Camp in a helicopter. Russell would have his regular team already established there. It would be an easy transition for the additional peaks since my team would be pulling out all our gear from Dhaulagiri.

That spring, we flew to Nepal, and I will never forget the feeling of total freedom. There were no clients, just us. We were free to trek and plan according to our schedule. We didn't need an elaborate base camp setup or fancy lodging. It was a stripped-down operation reminiscent of the old way adventurers used to climb.

In retrospect, Dhaulagiri was not the best selection as a return objective for Cecilie. Though she had climbed Manaslu since the K2 accident, it is a relatively safe mountain compared to the challenges presented by Dhaulagiri, which is a massive mountain with steep slopes and quite significant avalanche hazards on the lower and middle parts of the route. Nonetheless, we arrived at the base camp fully prepared to give it a solid effort.

It was unheard of to have Sherpas fixing rope for commercial purposes on a mountain outside of Everest during that time. So we were happy to know that the base camp had some solid climbers to collaborate with to try to establish the route.

We mainly joined forces with two groups of Italians that we felt were in the right place at the right time. Marco Confortola was there with a strong Sherpa partner. Marco had been on K2 during the 2008 season when Rolf died. He had reached the summit but lost most of his toes due to frostbite after being out in the elements for an extended period after the bottleneck serac collapse. Even sans toes, he was a powerful high-altitude climber, and Cecilie knew him from the K2 season. Another group of Italians was part of a private team led by Mario Panzeri and Giampaolo Corona, two strong climbers whom we shared many mid-afternoon wine and salami sessions with at base camp in between rotations.

We spent several weeks climbing up and down the mountain on acclimatization runs to the upper camps, carrying most of the gear. We had hired one Sherpa to climb with us on the lower mountain to assist with ferrying loads, but we were going light and as fast as possible for the most part. Things took a turn for the worse after one particularly hairy night at Camp Two.

It was situated at 21,654 feet on the northeast ridge, in a spot known to be dangerous. Unfortunately, the avalanche-prone east face, which gets wind-loaded snow accumulating on the slope, is the only place to rest on that part of the route. We had tucked our tent as close as possible to the ridge itself, next to a cornice, trying to stay on the ridge proper. Nonetheless, we spent a sleepless night together as small slides of snow sloughed off and hit the uphill side of our tent. It was terrifying to think that we could be swept down the mountain in the dark, especially for Cecilie. She was still suffering from memories of the K2 serac collapse, which swept Rolf off the mountain. That spot had been the location of several accidents involving experienced parties in the past and had a reputation we both knew well.

I felt terrible for bringing her there. The next morning, we descended to base camp for a rest, which was part of our planned acclimatization schedule. I could feel that Cecilie's vibe had changed. She would walk off and sit by herself. We hiked up to an overlook one day and had a heart-to-heart conversation about the conditions on the mountain and the risk involved in continuing to establish a route to the summit. She told me that she had decided to forgo any more climbing on Dhaulagiri and instead focus her attention on the Khumbu on the Everest/Lhotse plan. I understood this rationale and agreed.

It was getting to the midpoint of the season for Dhaulagiri and especially for the Everest area. Still, I focused on giving Dhaulagiri one more look personally. I went back up for a rotation to try to assist the other climbers in fixing rope along the northeast ridge and establishing Camp Three. If possible, I would stay and continue on the mountain, joining forces with the Italians on a hopeful summit bid. I spent another sleepless night in Camp Two.

Along with a small band of mixed-nationality climbers, I began to climb toward where we had planned to establish Camp Three. The weather and conditions proved very difficult. We only managed to get a few hundred meters up the route before being turned back.

As I descended back to base camp, I began to get a clear picture that this was not the year to be trying the mountain. It was time to support my partner and close this chapter on Dhaulagiri for the season. I dusted off the same decision-making process in my mind that I had used on K2 in 2006. The mountain would always be there. I opted instead to fly to the Khumbu and support Cecilie's goal.

We arranged for a helicopter pickup in two days from base camp and began to pack our duffle bags. That was when we got an unwelcome message from Russell in Everest Base Camp. He had made the tough and unprecedented decision to end his Everest trip due to conditions on the route that he and his team had deemed too dangerous. It threw our whole plan into disarray. We sent back a message that we were about to fly to base camp the next day and to please let us know what options we had. He informed us just to come over, and we could figure it then.

When we landed in Everest Base Camp, Russell had already started to pack up his tents and supplies. We didn't know if we were going to be able to climb. We had already paid for our permits and logistics support; it was an extraordinary situation. Due to timing and the challenges this presented, we decided to forgo the Everest part of the double climb and focus on climbing Lhotse.

Since Russell was not an option to support us, I walked over to talk with my friends Willie and Damien Benegas at their base camp. Their Sherpa logistics provider was the brother-in-law of my man, Tshering. They agreed to let us blend in with their Argentinean team's support package.

Since we had been climbing, we simply needed to get one last acclimatization rotation up to Camp Three, to prepare for a summit. We banded together with Tomas Ceppi and Luciano Badino, both guides from Aconcagua. They were there to try to climb Lhotse without oxygen, and I had worked with both of them before and was comfortable with them. Tomas has since become one of the leading guides working for my company. We have shared many crazy adventures throughout the years.

Because we were a bit low on time to climb an 8,000-meter mountain such as Lhotse, we decided to climb using oxygen to at least try to salvage a peak that season.

This was my second time climbing Lhotse, so I knew the route well, and the summit day went smoothly. We knew that we would climb around the body of a climber who had died only days earlier. He had simply sat down at the base of the final stretch of fixed lines to the summit and died. When we reached him, it made me a bit sad, but we pressed on. You never really get used to seeing dead climbers along the way on these mountains, but after you have done it many times, you become more desensitized to the odd feeling. We reached the top simultaneously with the Polish alpinist Kinga Baranowska, on a beautiful and calm morning in the sun. We all snapped photos to celebrate and made the long descent of rappels back down the mountain. For Cecilie, Lhotse was also the fifth 8,000-meter peak she had climbed, and, though we didn't know it then, it was her last.

There was a new focus building in her. The talk of starting a family had been a low-level conversation over quite some time, but we had never really made any specific plans. I knew this was a topic that was gaining momentum for her, but we skirted diving deep into it. The sailboat was going to be delivered very soon, and for right or wrong reasons, we both focused on that instead. Cecilie went with some friends for the initial trial sail in Les Sables-d'Olonne, France, while I left on some trip to god only knows where. When I returned, I heard that the boat was pretty impressive. The manufacturer needed to do the last interior tweaks, but it was now officially hers.

A few weeks later, we both went back to Les Sables-d'Olonne to take delivery of the sailboat named *Fryd*. The word *fryd* in Norwegian basically translates to "delight" or the feeling of happiness. That perfectly described the feeling of sleeping on the boat those first nights in the marina. There were a thousand little details to learn before we took her out of the safety of the harbor. For me, it was so interesting and exciting to take on the challenge.

Our goal was to move the boat from the Atlantic coast of France southward along the shores of Portugal and Spain and into the Mediterranean, where the sailing is more forgiving. This would provide us with time to learn the intricacies of the boat as well as many good places to dock before dealing with more significant seas. The other reason we wanted to have the *Fryd* in the Mediterranean was the access to the rock climbing areas that litter the coast of Spain, France, and Italy.

To reach the Atlantic tip of Spain at A Coruña, we would need to accomplish a crossing of the Bay of Biscay. The crossing is not to be taken lightly. It has a notorious history of challenging conditions, not exactly the ideal first challenge for novice sailors in a new boat.

While Cecilie was busy doing some speeches in Norway, I traveled to Les Sables-d'Olonne with a friend of ours, Petter Garshol. Petter was a retired former military and commercial airline pilot who owned an Ovni

39, the slightly smaller sister boat to *Fryd*. He was an experienced sailor, and we trusted him to captain her across the Bay of Biscay with me as his second mate. After several days of preparation, we set off into the rolling waves of the open Atlantic Ocean for a three-day crossing to A Coruña, Spain. It was exhilarating, and I loved this style of travel. We exchanged watches throughout the nights and days while the other person slept, and soaked up the beauty of the open waters. We were lucky, with favorable weather and sea conditions, and we crossed with no issues.

I then learned that Scandinavians have a tradition that, once the boat is safely tied up, you partake in shots of a Danish liquor called Gammel Dansk. At ten in the morning, a few shots of celebratory spirits and some local Spanish beers were just the ticket after the successful crossing. We walked the streets of the town and drank red wine. I was immediately hooked on the life of sailing.

Petter and I waited at A Coruña for Cecilie to fly in from Norway. Then the three of us had a joyous week sailing the boat down the coast, stopping to visit Porto and Lisbon in Portugal, before Petter needed to get back home. By then I felt confident that I could captain the boat the rest of the way around the bend and into the Gibraltar Straits.

Cecilie and I managed just fine on our own, hugging the coast in case of an issue. After one last night spent in Bolonia, Spain, we set out early in the morning to enter the Mediterranean Sea. As we sailed through the darkness around Tarifa, the sun began to rise, making the waters glow. To starboard, we could see Morocco in the distance. We pulled the mainsail down to keep control and rode the tides into the Straits. The Rock of Gibraltar slid by, and all too soon, we found ourselves in one of the most famous bodies of water on earth.

We were sold on the sailboat life. After reaching Marbella, we found a safe marina to dock *Fryd* at for several weeks while we returned to Norway and other work obligations. I could not wait to get back to her and would even take trips by myself to the marina. Any excuse I could find saw me heading south. The boat shone from all of the polishing I gave it.

Over the next year, we lived a back-and-forth life from all points around the world, mixing in weeks or even months away with just the two of us or with friends on *Fryd*. We moved the boat along the Spanish coast, making stops in small, nondescript cities for wine and tapas in tiny cafes. I did the most rock climbing I had in years. We got to know the towns of Malaga, Valencia, and Barcelona. It felt like my own "maiden voyage." The sailing and climbing were experiences enough, but the memories I made along the way were more important.

After Spain, we worked our way up the French coast. We made a crossing to the Iberian islands of Mallorca, Ibiza, and Menorca. Finally, we undertook a long crossing to the Italian island of Sardinia.

We both loved Sardinia for its raw beauty. Plus, we had again found a small town with a safe and relatively inexpensive marina in which we could keep *Fryd* for extended periods as we traveled back and forth to northern Europe. This was when things started to change in our relationship. While I loved being on the water, I felt the pull of the mountains again and planned a trip back to Pakistan to try to climb Gasherbrum 2 again. On the other hand, Cecilie was filming another TV show in Norway and still feeling the understandable urge to have a baby. We were moving in two different directions. We both knew it but couldn't bring ourselves to discuss it yet.

When the trip to Pakistan fell through due to visa issues, I reluctantly flew down to Sardinia to meet Cecilie and some friends on *Fryd*. I will never forget one friend saying to me, "Why would you want to go to Pakistan and sit on a mountain when you can be here?" They were probably right. Thus the challenge for a mountaineer. Sometimes you can't see the fantastic things right in front of you when a fire inside yearns inexplicably for the hardships of the high mountains.

CHAPTER SEVEN

Heartbreak Part 2

I HAD PIECED TOGETHER THE PERFECT SITUATION FOR A WANDERING mountain climber; it was more than I could have hoped for or imagined. I had a girlfriend accomplished in both the mountain and polar ski worlds, who made an extremely good living financially, which was more than I could say. We had a sailboat together, and I had the support and freedom from an understanding partner to go on adventures. It is hard to know why the fire to keep going for goals and risking everything always stays with you. Especially when you seemingly have everything you could have hoped for in life.

Cecilie was, for the most part, finished with what I would term big expeditions. She had climbed five 8,000-meter mountains, Everest and K2 included. She had skied coast to pole on unsupported and unassisted trips to the South and North Poles, and she was the only female in a very exclusive club known as the True Adventurers Grand Slam. We had skied across Antarctica, climbed both rock and ice, and had shared numerous sailing adventures. Now she had another goal in her life, one that had been coming more into focus the last few years. She wanted to have a baby.

I, on the other hand, had never really felt that urge to have children to any great extent. Sure, I thought about it from time to time, but it always seemed like something for the future. While I understand the ingrained instinct that many women, and men, have on the issue, it was always only of mild passing interest to me. Throughout my thirties, I never really thought at all about it.

But I had turned the corner into another decade, past the "over the hill" hump, and celebrated my fortieth birthday with Cecilie, Bjorn, and her sister's family in Oslo. On a tree-lined hill above the city, we drank excellent cocktails and enjoyed the moment. Cecilie had bought me a lovely watch to mark the occasion, and things were picture-book perfect.

There was, however, one thing that I could not get out of my mind—the North Pole.

I think that maybe inside of me, there was some deep feeling of needing acceptance. I needed to prove something to myself and everyone else in the world, the Norwegian old-school polar community, and maybe even Rolf. I needed to show that I had what it took to ski unsupported to the North Pole—widely regarded as one of, if not the most demanding expeditions in the world. It had shattered many people's dreams over the years. And it was a critical piece of a twelve-year journey I had been on without even knowing it.

In a mostly unplanned way, I had somehow stumbled into climbing the Seven Summits and then entered the elite world of polar explorers with my trip across Antarctica. This had been beyond my wildest dreams just a few years before. Now I wanted to join the most exclusive club out there, the True Adventurers Grand Slam. Only twelve people in the world had climbed the Seven Summits and skied from coast to the South Pole and the North Pole wholly unsupported and unassisted. If I could pull off that one last major piece, the North Pole, I would also be the first American to do the Grand Slam in that fashion. Cecilie was the only female in that club. I just had to do it.

She understood the feeling; she had been there. We began to discuss the two topics of having a child and the possibility of a North Pole trip at length. Both of us supported both issues, but clearly, each had his or her own order of importance. I suppose this is how tensions in relationships begin. Whether money, family commitments, feelings of being trapped, not happy with a career, or whatever the topics are, they slowly grind away at the individuals in a partnership.

Hell, I even began to privately think more about trying to climb all the remaining 8,000-meter peaks on top of somehow making a North Pole trip. Call me crazy; I couldn't help it. Though I didn't express this thought to Cecilie, it exacerbated the problems underneath the current. I had promised her I would never go back to K2 after the tragedy of 2008. But I had started to think about heading back to that dangerous mountain to try to climb it.

I have never been good at expressing my feelings in the relationships I've been in. Over time I have recognized that girlfriends often need to pull things out of me until I suddenly release all that I have been thinking. I think I have a passive-aggressive tendency, and I should have begun working on that much earlier in my life. Is hindsight fun or what?

Cecilie seemed to lose a bit of interest in traveling down to *Fryd* unless we were going to stay on the boat as a moveable cabin and go rock climbing most of the time. I got it. She loved to rock climb. It was one of the coping mechanisms she had begun to focus on to take her mind off the clock ticking inside of her. I was more interested in just doing slow, boring crossings from one place to the next. Although we did not plan to move the boat from Sardinia anytime soon, I found reasons to jet down to Italy to check on *Fryd*. Unlike earlier, when I was doing this out of excitement, now I was doing it to avoid the reality of our strained relationship.

Around this time, Cecilie got an excellent opportunity to do a new television show in Norway. It would be a reality-type competition show that blended adventure and tests of skill. The co-host on the show would be a Norwegian guy who had a pretty similar background as mine, Aleksander Gamme. I knew him because they had already done a TV show together while we were broken up, and so he was a friend of Cecilie's.

Much like the *Dancing with the Stars* saga, Cecilie became fully engrossed with the show, diving into a hectic schedule of meetings and production. She was often traveling around Norway to film episodes. Tensions were building more and more within our relationship once again.

I didn't have any real plan for a North Pole trip but knew that if there were any way to piece together a trip somehow, I would do it. I had talked with Eric a few times about potentially trying to make an unsupported coast to pole trip, something rarely done. Eric had already done two trips from Cape Discovery in Canada to the North Pole and a historic and quite epic summer trip from Russia with Lonnie Dupree. But those trips, which were brutally hard, had involved resupply drops of food and fuel. The idea of hauling all the supplies from the start was far worse.

At first, he didn't show much interest in going to the North Pole yet again, but the Arctic Ocean is in his blood. He had been harboring a secret urge to go back to try to tell the story, in photos and film, of the North Pole journey. Over time the idea to attempt an unsupported expedition together was gaining steam inside his head. Plus, the last time anyone had skied from Canada to the North Pole was in 2010, when Eric's Save the Poles trip occurred. The teams who had attempted it since had not been successful. Logistics were getting harder to arrange, and, more importantly, the ice on the Arctic Ocean was becoming less stable. There was less of it each summer.

The fact that the changing climate was having a severe impact on the Arctic Ocean sea ice had captivated Eric for a long time. Over his career, he had been very focused on tying environmental concerns into his expeditions to help raise awareness. As we circled the project, ideas started to take hold. I knew this might be the opportunity we were both looking for, and the spring of 2013 would be the perfect time to try to make it happen.

We figured that a trip like this still had a lot going for it from the standpoint of potential interest from sponsors and bolstering our outdoor careers. The conversation around climate change was beginning to gain even more mainstream attention, and the Arctic was one of the main areas of concern. If we could get funding to film the expedition, it would be an excellent opportunity to showcase the trip's difficulty as an overall objective and raise awareness on climate issues.

Always on the lookout for another expedition challenge, and with all these factors in play, Eric decided he was in if I was. I couldn't believe it. We agreed that we would try to do a coast to North Pole ski trip, unsupported and unassisted. It would be close to 500 nautical miles over the most unforgiving terrain on the planet. After we made the decision,

I remember waking up one night thinking one thought: "Shit, what did I just commit to?"

Despite that thought, I knew that if I was going to pull off the North Pole, I was off to a good beginning. I had managed to line up one of the best people in the world to undertake such a bold trip into the unknown. Plus, I was confident I would have financial support from sponsors and emotional support from Cecilie, who knew this was important to me.

We made a tentative plan for the spring of 2013 for the expedition. There were significant hurdles in front of us, as is always the case with polar expeditions. The $220,000 cost of the trip would be a real challenge to overcome, but we were sure we could raise the money needed via sponsorships. One of the main focuses for Eric was documenting the trip somehow. We made efforts to begin thinking of media partners. Filming an expedition like this would be a challenge, adding a layer of difficulty to an already arduous endeavor. But the chance to tell the story of the Arctic Ocean and share the experience with the world was tantalizing.

Then a major hurdle presented itself. Eric's wife Maria became pregnant with their first child. The timing of this little bundle of joy coming into the world would have coincided with the proposed expedition. A wayward adventurer who is seemingly always on thin ice with his partner (like me), Eric knew that it would not jive. We decided to postpone the trip until March 2014.

We knew that the ideal number of teammates for the trip would be three. There were several reasons for that, starting with cost. The major expense was tied in the flights to the starting point at Cape Discovery, Canada, and of course, the return flight from the North Pole. That alone would account for basically half of the overall expense. These are fixed-cost flights, so the cost is spread out more if split between more people. Also, just as important, three skiers could split up the weight of supplies but still sleep in one tent. There was also the social side of having three people for support, assistance through rough ice, and other obstacles that were sure to arise once we started.

We had a few people in mind for a potential third team member, but the list was pretty short when it came down to the right fit. You don't just propose it to your buddy who is kind of into the outdoors. Ideally, the person should have already skied extensively in Greenland, Norway, Antarctica, or somewhere else remote and wild. Or they needed to be a badass who you think could figure it out along the way after some training beforehand. Eric talked with Jimmy Chin, the mountain climber and photographer famous for many exploits, most notably directing the film *Free Solo*. He was interested, but in the end, the timing would not work. While I was in Nepal, for who only knows what mountain, I had pitched the idea to Edurne Pasaban, a Spanish female climber. She was about to become the first woman in the world to climb all the 8,000-meter peaks. People like her were always interested, but typically they didn't know that much about the North Pole or polar ski trips in general. So it was a stretch that never panned out.

From the standpoint of selling the idea for filming, it made sense to try to have a female on the team. It would make a more diverse group and create an interesting dynamic for a potential documentary. In the early stages of planning, I even pitched the idea to Cecilie. She kind of half-jokingly said she might be interested in going with us, but that faded as the reality set in. She had had her experience going to the North Pole. It was where Rolf had proposed to her, and it is a pain in the ass trip to do anytime. She came to her senses and told me, "I am not going back to the North Pole; this is your trip."

I was off on a few guided climbing trips during the winter of 2013 as we searched for partners, mostly revolving around gear companies and the broader market. Thankfully Eric had a bit more time to focus on his contacts. He got a meeting with the Discovery Channel and flew to New York to pitch the project. After a detailed slide show that presented the project, they agreed to partner with us. They were drawn to the multitudes of challenges the expedition would have to overcome and the real-life drama the story would show to viewers.

The executives at Discovery decided that the documentary would be a good fit for their Animal Planet outlet, as they wanted to get back to more real-life adventure shows. Eric and a lawyer we hired made a plan for funding from the network in exchange for the rights to the footage we would shoot. We now had a media partner that wanted us to film the expedition for a documentary, which added credibility and a better chance of selling other sponsors on the idea.

Slowly but surely, we accumulated an impressive list of sponsors to join our team. Many were already partners of ours, and the range of support was broad. Bergans of Norway, the company I was working for as an ambassador, agreed to be our gear and partial financial sponsor. Other companies including Mountain Safety Research, Sony, and Microsoft came on board in some form or fashion. We could feel the momentum building.

Unfortunately, this came at the cost of my relationship, which once again started to feel like it was on life support. Cecilie was busy doing her own thing with speeches, television, and work with her sponsors while I guided trips and mainly focused on the North Pole. We began to fall into a similar pattern of two ships passing in the apartment in Oslo.

I was focused on the trip, and she could see that I was stalling on any future talks about a family. I think it was around this time that she started mentally checking out of the relationship a little bit, and I do not blame her for it. Inside my mind, I was thinking, "Just let me do this last expedition, and then I will be ready." But I don't think I did a good job of expressing that to her. We started to discuss maybe spending a little time apart, and it all came to a head one day while we were cleaning the apartment. All the quiet tension that had been building between us bubbled up, and soon we were making comments to each other that neither of us really meant. I finally snapped and said, "Fine. I am booking a flight to Colorado," in the heat of the moment.

The idea that a separation may be the answer was a hard pill to swallow. Especially for people who genuinely love each other, it can be hard to admit it to yourself. We settled on a half-baked plan that I would go to Colorado to focus on training for the North Pole and the project as a whole while she would do her things. We never really defined our status. We just separated, each going their own way. The words "we are breaking up" never left our mouths, but we decided not to be together for a while, with no set date to reunite.

It was so hard to pack my things. I kept asking myself if I was making the biggest mistake of my life. All the time and energy I had put into the relationship hung over me as I filled my duffel bags again. All I could think about was our experiences together and the seemingly perfect situation we had as a couple with mutual interests and lifestyles.

It was depressing in many ways to land back in the United States. Once again I was homeless, looking for an apartment to set up my temporary base. I felt like a cartoon character with a cloud hanging over my head. But at the same time, there was an undercurrent of excitement. I was back in Boulder, where the adventure world resides in the United States. My smile brightened as I walked down Pearl Street, affectionately known as the "Rodeo Drive of outdoor companies." I was surrounded by a community that embraced the need to go exploring, and that helped. It felt easier to train, meet with companies, and make contacts for the North Pole trip, which was drawing closer by the day.

By now, the idea of finding the perfect third person to join the expedition was waning. I had asked Bjørn Sekkesæter, with whom I had skied across Greenland, if he had any interest, which I knew he did. But he had to say no; he had family and work commitments. So Eric and I decided to make the trip as a simple two-person team.

Cecilie and I called each other periodically to check in, but it was a strange situation. I could hear in her voice that she was a bit lost, probably the same way I was feeling. But my focus now was on a major expedition, so it was easier to concentrate on that and not on personal life matters. One of the memories I have that still bothers me to this day happened over Christmas in 2013. As I recall, Cecilie had traveled to Thailand to go rock climbing with a bunch of Norwegian friends. She sounded despondent when we talked. We cried and discussed what was going on in our worlds. I was sitting in my dad's office, and around me were books and pictures of Antarctica and little memorabilia from our trip together. I distinctly remember finally saying to her, "Maybe it is better for us to be together." But neither of us acted on that feeling, and it just drifted away. When I hung up the phone, I felt so empty.

As the spring approached, Eric and I focused on training as much as we could. We were both busy with random short trips and our own commitments. Still, we managed to piece together a schedule of training in and around Boulder. We had not done much training together over the years. Once, Eric had traveled to Norway when I was still living there, and we had flown up to Svalbard to ski on a mini-expedition with sleds and most of the gear we would use on the actual trip. But we never got out on any sea ice, something I knew worried Eric.

I think he had a lot of faith in assuming we would make a great team on the Arctic Ocean. But the dynamic environment of floating sea ice is quite different from anything else on the planet. He viewed my polar ski experience on Greenland and Antarctica as a foundation for the epic we were committed to in the Arctic. Still, I knew he wished we had time on actual sea ice to get our systems dialed in.

All we could do was focus on getting physically ready for the incredible rigors presented on an unsupported North Pole trip. So we set about trying to get "old man strong." It is hard to describe the training you need to do in preparation for a trip across the Arctic Ocean. The simple answer is you need to be strong everywhere. We would be skiing hours on end, day after day during marathon travel sessions, so arriving in good cardiovascular shape was a must. But we would also face fifty-plus days of pulling heavy sleds over colossal ice chunks, shoveling snow, and setting up camp over and over and over again—all in an incredibly unforgiving frozen environment.

Eric and I would meet and do hikes on the mountain trails around Boulder with heavy backpacks, the only criteria being to go uphill fast. This built overall strength and also taxed our cardio levels. Riding bikes for hours on end also strengthened our leg muscles. But the most crucial aspect of our training was becoming great friends with two large truck tires.

The trick is to try to mimic the actions you would do on the trip. So we would each pull two truck tires, using our polar harness, up and down hills for hours. That fired up the core muscles and got them ready for pulling a 320-pound sled over rough terrain. Then we would carry, flip, and beat those tires mercilessly with sledgehammers. Those poor tires, what did they ever do? People must have thought we were nuts as they hiked past us on walks with their dogs. You get all kinds of funny looks and questions when you are dragging tires along trails, such as "What are you doing, training for something?" Or "Are you guys grooming the gravel trails?" If we felt like getting into a conversation, we would answer that we were training for the North Pole. But typically that would elicit too many questions, so we usually merely said we were getting in shape for a trip.

Animal Planet had arranged for a production company called High Noon Entertainment to do the documentary filming that would take place in Boulder before the trip. Eric was on as a producer, and he did a fantastic job of putting all the pieces together for the filming project. We kind of felt like movie stars, albeit minor ones.

Eric was focused on the documentary side of things, as this was one of the crucial reasons for the trip. He had skied to the North Pole three times prior, but this trip was the chance to showcase the journey to the world and highlight the importance of the Arctic Ocean. I was excited about the documentary, but Eric gets the credit for putting it all together and becoming proficient in filming.

High Noon had an office in Denver, so it was easy for us to arrange filming times in Boulder. They came to Boulder with a crew several times to set up pre-trip interviews, film us testing gear and pulling tires to train, and generally get our impressions on the upcoming expedition. I have to say they did a fantastic job of capturing the pre-trip jitters and excitement.

Once we departed to Canada, however, it would be up to Eric and me to film the actual expedition. This only added another layer of challenge to an already tricky endeavor.

As the expedition approached, the stress level went into overdrive. We were still beating the bushes to find the final funding we needed to pay the flight company for the reserved flights in advance. Everything seemed to be expensive, from the battery budget to the shipping of sleds to Resolute, Canada in advance of the trip. We split up the to-do list and maxed out our credit cards to try to get each item checked off.

Luckily, Cecilie had lent us her and Rolf's Acapulka North Pole sleds. That saved us from spending 7,000 Euros, money we quickly spent elsewhere. Getting those sleds to Resolute was on my checklist, and it was a frustrating ordeal to find a reliable way to ship them there in advance. Every option seemed crazy expensive, and I was stressed. When

I told Eric about my plight with the sleds, he merely replied, "Figure it out." That was his way of saying, "I don't know, I have my own shit to deal with right now." Our days consisted of arranging thousands of details, every one of them extremely important either to the trip's outcome or our survival.

I finally figured it out, and we shipped the sleds and part of our gear northward. Another item on my checklist was the task of re-sealing every seam on our waterproof dry suits. We would be using the suits to swim across open water leads in the pack ice, and a leak discovered on the ice could be life-threatening. This tedious but essential task was the bane of my existence for about four days. It caused me to miss two haircut appointments before the departure date. My very busy hairdresser then stopped taking my calls and broke off our relationship. It seemed that the trip was wreaking havoc on all my personal connections.

We had a series of flights that would take us through stops in Canada until ultimately landing in Resolute, departing on the last day in February. During that final week, we had a substantial invoice due to Kenn Borak Air. They are the flight operator well known for ferrying scientists and wayward adventurers around the Arctic and were the only option for getting us to the starting spot at Cape Discovery. Luckily for us, we had learned that two Norwegians were also going for the North Pole, and we arranged to share the flight from Resolute to the starting point with them. That effectively halved the $45,000 flight. But we still had to prepay the $110,000 return flight from the North Pole back to Resolute. They would send a plane to pluck us off the ice when we either made the Pole or decided we were finished. There was no negotiating on this one.

The financial costs associated with the trip felt like playing a game of Whac-A-Mole. As soon as we paid for one thing, another would pop up. Using the funding raised through the myriad of sponsors and Animal Planet, and the substantial amount of cash both Eric and I put into the budget, we had managed to gather almost all the money needed for the flights. But we still had a $20,000 gap left, and neither Eric nor I had any option left to borrow the money, as we had both gone to the extremes of our finances.

I made a last-ditch call to my brother Tate. Of course, my family knew about the trip but did not have a good grasp on the behind-the-scenes costs involved. I just came out and asked Tate, "Hey, what do you think of sending me a cashier's check tomorrow for $20,000?" In a show of total support and confidence, he hung up the phone and drove to the bank. We had our final funding in place and sent a wire to Kenn Borak for $130,000. Talk about stress.

Those last two days were a blur of activity. We still had to pack a mountain of freeze-dried dinners for the entire expedition, around 110 of them. And to make matters worse, in true dirtbag fashion, I had decided to move out of the apartment I was living in before we left Boulder. I figured two months of rent could go a long way toward hotel costs in Resolute, so it made sense to me. I shuttled clothes, a bed, furniture, and a ton of gear to a storage unit and asked Eric if I could stay at his house the night before our flight from Denver. Looking back on that now, I am sure he and Maria didn't love the idea. It was their last night together for over two months; I am sure they would have liked to spend it alone. It didn't matter anyway; there was no sleep that night as we finished the thousandth detail.

The next morning, we were picked up by a massive SUV and loaded around ten duffle bags in the back. I called Cecilie one last time and tried to express my feelings as best I could. I watched Eric, who had a family, hugging important people goodbye. I went to the airport as a solo traveler. Once again, I wondered what I was sacrificing in my life in pursuit of adventure. Cecilie wished me luck and asked that I send her messages along the way. She was there to support me from afar in any way possible.

I was nervous but excited about the adventure and the challenge that lay ahead. I knew it would be the hardest thing I had ever attempted, but I would do the best I could. I had done many big expeditions by this time, so I was used to the nagging feeling that some detail was forgotten, or something had been left out of a duffle bag. But everything had been triple-checked, and it was time to take three flights over the next twenty-four hours to reach the staging town at Resolute.

We dropped into the lounge at the airport to partake in a nerve-relaxing Bloody Mary in hopes of actually sleeping on the plane.

There is a point in expeditions when you are relieved to board the plane because there is nothing left to do at that point. You can turn on a movie, zone out, and forget about the lists for a while. After weeks of stress and wrangling for money, Eric and I were fried mentally. But to say we were excited about the upcoming expedition would have been an understatement.

As we took off north toward Canada, I stared out the window and reflected on my long journey through the Seven Summits, many Himalayan adventures, and crossing Antarctica. I had no idea if we would be successful on this, the hardest of all trips, but I had a quiet confidence in our small team. I had had a similar feeling when Cecilie and I skied across Antarctica. On that trip, I knew as long as nothing happened that was out of our control, nothing could stop us. The problem was that we were walking into a place where almost everything is out of your control, and seemingly everything is trying to stop you.

CHAPTER EIGHT

The Absurdity of It All

As I skied out across the meager one-inch-thick layer of bending ice, it miraculously held tension over the 29-degree water of the Arctic Ocean. I tried hard not to remind myself that the sea beneath us was 14,000 feet deep. No one would willingly cross such thin ice towing a loaded sled behind them in normal circumstances, but these were not normal times. I was on the polar ice sheet and about to get my first introduction to something that would become terrifyingly common on our trip—crossing a lead on the ice.

A lead or a crack in the ice is a dangerous roadblock that occurs when the pans of ice floating on the surface of the water separate. When this happens, it reveals what is really going on beneath your feet. The seemingly solid surface of ice that you are standing on is, in reality, just large sheets of ice that move along at the mercy of tides, wind, and currents in the water below. We were merely passengers in this floating environment and at its mercy.

We had come across our first lead the day before and decided to put up camp. We were hoping it would refreeze overnight when the temperatures plummeted below freezing. That would allow us to travel forward in a straight line to the north instead of skiing far out of our intended direction to execute an end run around the massive lead, which stretched into the horizon in both directions, disappearing into the winter haze.

In the morning after a cold evening, the cracks or leads we encountered would either be a thin new layer of ice, a slushy mess in the process of refreezing, or simply open water. That was the reason we had brought two dry suits along. They would allow us to swim from one side of the lead to the other if necessary. Something we hoped to avoid as much as possible.

When the frozen layer of ice was thin, an experienced polar eye was needed to test the tension and stability to see if it was possible to ski across. Eric had the Arctic experience, so I deferred to him. When we returned to the edge to test the ice in the morning, it seemed pretty solid, albeit a tad flexible. Eric gave the ice a few sharp taps with his ski pole tip and declared it skiable. "Well, I think we will chance it," he said that frosty morning. To which I replied, "I like the word *chance* thrown in there." I trusted his judgment but was still nervous.

The whole lead was around fifty yards or more to cross, the distance a football will travel when tossed by an NFL quarterback. Eric skied out, pulling his sled behind him, and made easy progress at first. As he got farther out, toward the middle of the frozen lead, it was my turn to go. Eric appeared to be nearing a section of more stable multi-year ice on the other side, so I gingerly started forward. I stopped at the edge to quickly survey the best route to take. I didn't want to ski on his track since it was already degrading the surface. I could see that the closer he got to the safety of the other side of the lead, his ski track was beginning to fill with water seeping in from below the thin sheet of ice.

As I moved forward, I watched out of the corner of my eye as Eric adjusted his technique. He was desperately widening his gait and ski pole placement to try to spread his weight over the ice surface. He narrowly made it to the safety of the solid ice on the other side of the lead. I was still out in the middle. I had no choice but to continue forward, with an eye focused on the edge of safety, trying to sneak across the bending ice below my skis.

In my mind, I needed to look for a better way across the final stretch, but this thought was tempered by the obvious fact that I needed to get the hell off this thin ice and to the other side quickly. Eric unhooked from his sled and started to ski close to where I would exit from my precarious location. "Just go, goddammit, don't stop," he yelled. I was a mere five yards away from safety when the ice below my skis deteriorated.

A slow, sinking feeling overtook me. My skis disappeared into the water as the ice gave way. I was in the water up to my ankles but could move forward just a bit more, then the whole thing gave way, and I was in the ice-cold Arctic Ocean up to my chest.

All I could think was, "Don't lose your skis." Have you ever tried to swim with skis on your feet? It's not easy, and I was scared as hell, but I couldn't let the danger I was in cloud my actions. I tried to remain calm as I slowly dog-paddled toward the edge of the solid pan of ice. Luckily I made it to the edge of good ice and, using the sharp tips of my ski poles as polar picks, was able to climb out on the other side with all my gear intact.

The problem was, I was soaking wet, and the ambient air temperature was 30 degrees below zero. I needed to get out of my soaked clothing fast. Eric dove into my sled, looking for my emergency clothes bag. At the same time, I stripped down to my wool underwear layers, shedding my rapidly freezing outerwear. We each had an emergency stuff sack prepped with new base layers for just this kind of situation. He found my bag of clothes and tossed it to me. I gratefully shed my wet base layer and pulled on fresh clothes while Eric anxiously looked on, offering me reassurances that things would be fine. He told me to just focus on getting warm. I did jumping jacks and ran around trying to rewarm myself; it was scary. Call it a numb mind from many dangerous situations on other adventures, or maybe just too many days living at high altitude, but I blacked out the danger and instinctively did what needed to happen.

Because it was midday and the weather was luckily very "nice," we decided to keep skiing the rest of the day. If the weather had been worse, I could have been in serious trouble. But that day, there was no reason to stop, and the minutes were too valuable. It just meant I would have to endure the rest of the day skiing in frozen boots and outerwear. Such is life on a North Pole expedition.

One could argue that the trip had begun with all the preparations back in Colorado, but the actual expedition had started when we reached Resolute, Canada. It's a tiny Inuit village perched on the edge of nowhere with a population of 240 souls. Calling it the last place on earth would not be too much of a stretch. The ironically named South Camp Inn was our refuge in the middle of a harsh, cold landscape. As the only place to stay in town, it had seen a fair amount of adventurers over the years. We were one of four teams staying there that year; all of us were going for the Pole. Luckily our sleds had arrived without any issues beforehand, something that tends to get screwed up more often than not. The inn had a huge meeting room that was perfect for spreading out your gear to do the final packing in preparation for a flight to the starting line at Cape Discovery. So we divided up the room and got to work.

Our flight to Cape Discovery, on the northern end of Ellesmere Island, where we would enter the polar ice pack, was scheduled for March 7, five days off. But we still had a hundred things left on the checklist, everything from little clothing and gear tweaks—such as making our face coverings, called nose beaks, that were sewn on our goggles—to finalizing our boot systems with the insulated outer boots and such. We needed to get everything finished to do a run-through sled packing day to see how the loads would fit and carry. On top of all the gear work, we still had about a day's worth of food preparation. We needed to cut fifty salami and cheese lunch packs for each of us, make breakfasts ready to go each morning with precise measurements of ingredients, and load the pre-packed dinners into stuff sacks. Organizing our fourteen gallons of fuel into canisters and MSR fuel bottles was also of critical importance. Each piece, no matter how seemingly small, was crucial to do correctly. There is absolutely no room for error on the Arctic Ocean, and we had a constant feeling of stress while preparing.

The first two expeditions to try for the Pole were a solo Japanese skier named Yasu Ogita and the Irish duo of Clare O'Leary and Mike O'Shea. They were scheduled for the first flight to Cape Discovery and had been at the South Camp Inn prepping for a couple of days prior to our arrival. The third team was the Norwegians Lars Fleslan and Kristoffer Glestad, with whom we planned to share our flight. When the first flight took off in clear weather and a good forecast, we were happy and hoped the weather would cooperate for us. Of course it didn't.

As we got closer to the day of departure, Eric and I felt pretty good about our systems, though it always felt like there was much more to do. So fate decided to give us more time, much more than we wanted.

We received news on the night of March 6 that there was a bad weather system that would prevent us from flying.

We ended up getting delayed by a week for our flight. Lousy weather had moved into the area. It was not a big deal at the beginning, as it allowed us some extra time to finish things. But as the days stretched longer, we started to get stressed. We had finished every last detail and had nothing left to do except wait. It sucked. I even did my taxes one day after we disappointedly heard there would be no flight that day. I sent the information to my accountant, who was amazed at the unexpected arrival of documents from the middle of nowhere. With each day's delay, we were in danger of having to cancel the expedition before it ever started. Kenn Borek Air had a hard deadline for the last day they would fly up to retrieve anyone from the ice. We were reaching a tipping point of not having enough days to realistically reach the North Pole, which meant it would be pointless to start. Not to mention that each night was costing us $200 to stay in the hotel, money we didn't have. Out came our credit cards, and the debt continued. It was a stressful time.

On the evening of March 14, we finally received a bit of good news; the weather looked suitable for a flight in the morning.

We met the Norwegians at the airplane hangar and loaded up for the shared flight. We flew for several hours, making a short but brutally cold stopover at the not-so-bustling airport at the Eureka weather station. The average low temperature there in March is minus 40.3 degrees F. Waiting on the tarmac, it was epically cold. Eric and I ran around in circles to try to stay warm as the pilots refueled the plane. We noted that the Norwegians just stood there, and we could not figure out how they were not getting cold—especially with their sleek boot systems. The warmth of the plane was glorious when we climbed back in for the final stretch of flying to the northern end of Ellesmere Island. The scenery was breathtaking. As we approached the end of the mountains that marked the edge of the land, it was otherworldly. I looked north toward the Arctic Ocean; there was only an endless expanse of white jumbled ice.

After taking a couple of test landings, the Kenn Borek pilots landed the Twin Otter ski-equipped plane on the ice. As the door to the plane opened, the cold snapped us to attention. We unloaded the two teams' worth of gear quickly and set about readying the sleds as our breath billowed around us in the frigid air. The pilots were keen to take off and head back, so we had to be efficient in our movements. They shot a quick photo of us and then climbed into their warm cockpit for the trip south.

After the plane had left and we were alone there in the silence of the edge of the world, reality set in. Nothing left to do but start skiing. Eric and I were psyched to get going; the clock was ticking. The Norwegians skied off into the horizon with lighter sleds than us, and we commented to each other on how efficient their setup seemed. We were the old-school guys, each pulling a heavy 317-pound sled. The hill that led down from the mainland toward the edge of the sea ice was pleasant, but that all changed once we hit the rough pressure ice waiting for us.

From where we stepped onto the ocean to the geographic North Pole at 90 degrees north latitude is approximately 420 nautical miles. Each degree of latitude consists of 60 nautical miles. We began our journey at 83 degrees north latitude, which meant we had 7 degrees to cover. In the big picture of the entire expedition, if we were to try to break the speed record of forty-nine days, that meant we would need to average just over 8.57 nautical miles or better per day. On our first day out in the harsh terrain of jumbled ice and extreme cold, we covered 1.16 nautical miles. The ice was brutal, unlike anything I had encountered in Antarctica or on other trips with Cecilie.

The reality was harsh. Keeping in mind that I had known all the challenges that came with an unsupported trip to the North Pole, it was still way harder than I expected. Eric had been here before, albeit with a lighter sled on two supported trips, and the weight and challenge of moving the sleds through the rough ice was like a slap in his face too. As far as the eye could see across the horizon was rough-pressured ice with massive blocks of it piled high into the air. We knew it would be tough going for a long time. Nothing would get easy until we hopefully broke free onto larger pans of ice that would allow us to make greater distances. But that was in the future. We knew from the start that we would have to play major league catchup later in our average daily distance covered to be successful.

In many ways, the mental challenges of that first week exceeded the physical. However, the physical part was the hardest thing I had ever experienced. We labored day in and day out in the low light and early spring cold of the Arctic. Each morning was a challenge to psych yourself up enough to unzip the sleeping bag in the ice-laden humidity of the tent and start a new day of struggle. Somehow we managed, over and over again. The added pressure of filming these daily efforts was a balance that we needed to find between us. In my mind, I was focused on continuously moving forward, and Eric was too, but we also had to film the trip. We had to stop to set up cameras, ski through the frame, and then go back and collect the equipment to do it all over again. It was a tricky balance.

To date, only forty-seven people had ever skied unsupported and unassisted to the North Pole. The first Americans to complete the journey unsupported were John Huston and Tyler Fish in 2009, completing the journey in fifty-four days. Virtually all had used a two-sled system—one longer and one shorter sled loaded with gear that were hooked into a line to be pulled together on clear ice but separated in more complex conditions. The idea in difficult conditions is that you pull one sled forward a certain distance and then return for the second sled to repeat the route. Thus you had two sleds of manageable weight that you could move forward. Over the course of the expedition, your supplies would dwindle to the point where you could begin using just the larger sled, and the small sled would be abandoned.

Eric and I had decided to use just one large sled each, fully loaded, and we knew the disadvantages. In the beginning, the sleds would be super heavy and hard to move and maneuver, but we didn't like the idea of leaving a sled behind on the ice. Plus, we had saved some money since Cecilie had loaned us her sleds. We figured that things would get easier once we burned through some supplies and got farther out on the ice, where historically there were long stretches of smoother ice. We came to rue this decision.

We soon realized that the best way to deal with the sleds was for both of us to clip into one and pull it forward together before returning to retrieve the other sled. Unfortunately that meant we were doing double duty. We managed to battle through the first week, covering roughly six nautical miles. It was depressing and created a lot of anxiety when thinking about the reality of reaching the Pole. The distances were overwhelming. That's when things got a bit more interesting.

The expedition was hard enough with the cold, wind, rough surface, and physical strain. The last thing we needed was to be hunted by the largest carnivore on four legs on the planet, but that was the next little wrinkle in our daily struggle.

We were both clipped into Eric's sled, pulling it forward onto an open section of ice about 600 feet away. My sled was left behind for the next trip. I am not sure why we stopped right when we did, but it was a miracle in disguise. As we huddled together, giving each other single words of praise between panting breaths, we unclipped from the sled and turned around to start back for the other one. It took a moment to realize that a mother polar bear and her cub were directly behind us, no more than thirty feet away, walking straight toward us in the track we had just laid out.

My breath disappeared, and my first instinct was to raise my poles and shout, which was the wrong thing to do, according to what Eric had taught me. I stood mesmerized for a moment while they briefly paused; maybe our turning around had confused them. Eric jumped into action and frantically screwed on a pencil flare that both of us were carrying in our pants thigh pocket. He shot the little cracker flare at the heads of the oncoming bears. I was busily cross-threading my tiny flare onto the device, a few seconds behind him. All I could think was, "Shit, why are these so small?" Eric's flare stopped them for a brief moment. Their small black noses were raised in the air, sniffing for scents, trying to figure out what these oddly colored and smelly things were walking out on the ice. We sure were funny-looking food to them. They slowly started to walk toward us again.

I finally was able to shoot my flare at their heads, which caused them to pause again. Our frantic but relatively controlled response finally paid off when Eric was able to reach into the sled and pull out our pistol grip shotgun. (We just happened to be pulling the sled that had our firearm in it, a fifty-fifty chance.) He fired off a bear scare round directly at their heads. The first two rounds in the chamber were nonlethal flares designed to scare off bears without harming them. The third round in the shotgun was a lethal round, and we certainly were hoping not to use that, but would if we needed to.

The mother polar bear turned tail and ran away, and the cub followed in her tracks. Eric and I let out a nervous laugh of fear. "Holy shit, dude!" I believe we both said simultaneously. We took a moment to collect ourselves and then began to walk toward my sled to retrieve it. That's when we discovered that the two bears had been following us for around a thousand feet, walking directly behind us. At any moment, the mother could have closed the distance and taken a swipe with her gigantic paw as we struggled with the sled. It would have been the beginning of a gruesome scene that most likely would have ended with two dead polar adventurers. From that day on, whenever we pulled just one sled forward, we moved the gun with us.

The daily grind began to take its toll early on as we struggled to escape the rough ice that was attached to the land for miles. The fight each day was disheartening. We had to scout the route in advance to find the "best" way northward on the compass bearing, which devoured time and energy. We knew we had to make more distance if there was going to be any chance of reaching our goal. But both of us were experienced enough to know that we had to compartmentalize those issues and focus on each day, not the overall journey. Just keep moving forward became my mantra.

We were reminded of the reality of the Arctic when on a radio call we learned that one team had to abandon their trip. The Norwegian team had been evacuated due to frostbite on all their toes. The Arctic Ocean is an unforgiving place, and this was just par for the course. We also wondered about the thinner boots they had been wearing and seriously pondered if waiting on the runway at Eureka had anything to do with it? Possibly the damage had started there—it was that cold. We were sad to hear about their departure but got back to business the next day.

A couple of weeks into the expedition, we slowly could see that we were getting onto more-stable and larger pans of ice. The soul-crushing jumble of pressure ice was lessening as we moved farther out on the ocean, and soon we were able to make some good distance each day.

One day as we trudged along, we were surprised by the low engine rumble of a Twin Otter plane high above us. We figured that maybe someone had decided to get a resupply or something like that, but we would later find out that somewhere ahead of us there had been another evacuation. The Irish team had an accident involving a sled falling on a team member, and they had decided it was too dangerous to continue. That left just Yasu and Eric and me, the only three humans within hundreds if not a thousand miles in any direction. It was a harrowing thought, one that stuck with me as I battled forward each day.

One of the biggest interpersonal struggles for our team involved the juxtaposition of moving forward at every moment with stopping to film those movements. It is common to have interpersonal struggles on expeditions. No matter how good of friends you are, it just happens. Eric was keenly focused on getting footage and photos, while I was more focused on momentum. Though we both were committed to the trip for the same overall reason, we each had a specific purpose that drove our motivation under the surface. Eric wanted to tell the fantastic story on film, and I wanted to reach the North Pole by any means possible to become the first American to complete the Grand Slam with unsupported and unassisted ski trips. Eric, with his extensive experience, was making the vast majority of our big decisions. But he was also heavily focused on the filming, and that was wearing on me. I found it stressful to stop to film and take pictures. Tensions began after less than a week out on the ice.

We had to figure out a balance together, because there was starting to be real friction between us. In the tent each night, we would hardly talk. We would, of course, discuss the essentials such as distance, time, fuel, and so on, but not much else besides an occasional complaint. There was always something to be doing, even in the tent at night. We had to make water, call in dispatches, charge batteries, fix gear, and sometimes even doctor ourselves. The wall of drying clothes hanging from the inside of the tent essentially separated us as we tried to rest for the next day's efforts.

Both of us were highly experienced on expeditions, and we knew we had to fix the issue of our overall working relationship. I totally agreed with Eric's point of view; I knew we needed to film, and more importantly, I needed to do more of my part in filming. We had several meetings over a few nights and discussed how we could manage things better. I consciously decided I needed to up my game on the camera side and help with the footage instead of dreading it. Things started to get better after that, and we could face little challenges on the route as a team again. We were actually laughing now and again at the challenges of each day.

One of those challenges was sleeping. It was not an option to just dive into a fluffy, minus-40-degree down sleeping bag and call it a day. The extreme cold and humid environment called for a precise sleeping system that Arctic adventurers have perfected over the years.

We employed a three-bag system. The outermost layer was a synthetic-filled minus-20-degree sleeping bag, which provided the first, outer line of warmth but was primarily needed to keep moisture off the more important inner down sleeping bag. Moisture is your enemy inside the tent. Steam from water heating on the stove is quite dangerous. We tried to minimize the problem by carefully monitoring the water pot as it approached the boiling point, turning the stove off before lots of steam came out. Plus, the moisture from our breath would almost instantly freeze inside the tent.

The next sleeping bag was a fluffy minus-40-degree down bag. We slept inside a vapor barrier liner, the third bag, designed to keep the moisture coming from our body away from the down sleeping bag. The whole system was closed off, and only a tiny hole within the tunnel of the down sleeping bag face tube allowed in any fresh air. It was so cold we couldn't expose any skin to the night air, so we had to sleep with balaclavas covering our face. When I woke up in the morning and looked at the inside of the tent, covered in huge, delicate ice crystals from our breath, and at Eric swaddled inside so many layers, sometimes I couldn't help but laugh. Then I realized I had to leave the warmth and dive into the cold.

A North Pole expedition has a way of boiling down essential things in everyday life. You are struggling all the time and getting worn down to the core. I was thinking a lot about Cecilie and wondered how she had felt at this point on her own North Pole expedition so many years before. I typed a message to her on my satellite phone, saying that I felt like I was going to be "done" after this trip, and I would be ready for the next steps in life, which would include the things that had been so important to her at the time of our separation. The next day I got a cheery message back from her in support, saying she knew what I was going through and to just keep going. But there was no response to the other things I had mentioned. I took it for what it was worth. People back in the real world who knew what we were going through did not want to create more drama in any way, only words of support.

When we reached day twenty-five of the expedition, basically half the time we had allotted to reach the North Pole, we had only managed to cover 86 nautical miles. That meant we still had 334 nautical miles to cover in the same amount of time. That put into perspective the overwhelming odds we were facing on our race to the Pole. We started to have frank conversations in the tent at night about whether we would even be able to get to the Pole with the number of days left.

To make it, we knew that we simply had to start making more distance each day—close to six or seven nautical miles a day for the next week to even have a chance at making our goal. The odds would be against us. But we knew that later in the trip, as our sleds got to their lightest weight and we reached the projected better ice with large, flat pans, we could potentially cover upward of fifteen to seventeen nautical miles in a day. It would come down to the law of averages. There was no other way to get to the North Pole other than to put our heads down and move forward.

We had started our ski journey at the 83rd parallel, and after eighty-six nautical miles we had only reached 84.47 degrees. The thought of covering over 5 degrees of latitude in such a short amount of time was overwhelming mentally. So we had no choice but to focus on short-term goals instead of the big overall picture. We decided that our near-term goal was to reach the 87th parallel, and then we would reassess our situation and make a new goal at that point.

Though we now had a plan in place, the environment was not buying into it. We ran into day after day of whiteout conditions. The way you make a lot of distance in a single day is to have good surface conditions and clear weather. Even having one of those two factors allows you to move efficiently. We didn't have either.

If the surface of the ice was smooth, or if we were on big, flat pans of ice or a system of frozen leads heading in the general correct direction, visibility was not that big a deal. We could just ski through the muck following a compass bearing. Conversely, if the weather was clear, it was much easier to ski around obstacles in our way and move on down the road, as it were.

Our problem was that we ran into bad weather and poor conditions on the ice. We were forced to battle the elements day in and day out for around a week, fighting for distance northward. It was windy, cold (around 40 degrees below zero), and totally demoralizing. The physical toll was weighing heavily on our bodies each day, and we were losing weight. We had upped our caloric intake by 2,000 calories per day for this section of the trip but were still at a deficit overall. The cold wasn't helping. It burned more calories, sapped our energy, and generally made even the simplest things hard to do.

We had another factor that was beginning to creep into the equation. The ice pans we were traveling on had started to drift south at a more rapid pace. The pattern is well known, and we expected this to happen. As you reach the area closer to the North Pole, the ice starts to drift south toward northern Canada and Greenland, which is not a big issue during the day when you are skiing northward, though it is always in the back of your mind that the ice you are on is working against you with each step.

It is more significant at night. Not only were we fighting the elements and the clock ticking, but once we put up the tent and crawled in, we drifted backward for twelve hours while we ate, prepared, and slept. Each morning we would wake up and check the GPS to see how many hard-fought miles from the day before we had lost simply by sleeping.

On day thirty-six of the expedition, we had reached fifteen nautical miles into the 86th parallel. We had been swapping shifts out front, navigating in the morning, and making our way around some big pressure ice (which forms when two ice sheets crash together into nasty ridges of broken ice, often many feet high and never-ending). On the ice surface, we started to see something quite peculiar. It appeared like there were ski tracks. It made no sense. The tracks were heading in the general direction we were traveling, so we followed alongside them for a few hundred meters to see what was going on. We came around a giant ice chunk, and there was a tent on the ice. It was surreal. At first it didn't register, but after a quick discussion, we determined that it must be Yasu, the solo Japanese skier. It was crazy to think that out here, in the middle of nowhere, we should happen across the only other person still here.

We skied up to his tent, and Yasu popped his head out with a greeting. He had been sitting in his tent for a couple of days and had decided to give up on his bid to reach the Pole. He told us he was low on fuel and generally unable to progress forward anymore, so he had called Kenn Borek for a pickup. He would need to wait for several more days for good weather. There was not much we could do or say but give him our best and keep skiing. So we bid him farewell, he wished us luck, and we continued on our way. From that point on, we would be alone.

The next forty-five nautical miles were a blur of daily toil, both physical and emotional. During that time, we were fighting the battles of homesickness and the doldrums of being neither here nor there. We were past the middle point but still so far away from the end. Eric was battling some emotional challenges missing his family. I completely understood. I was also missing my loved ones and the comforts of home. But I did not have a wife and child, so I tried to be compassionate to his situation. He would be in a bad mood each morning, and it was starting to weigh on our trip. Finally, I flatly said to him, "You can't get more news from home that is negative. You need to dial it in and be here now." This was not some clairvoyant experience I had from previous Arctic expeditions. We both were veterans of numerous expeditions and knew the challenges we were facing. The only way we could overcome the hurdles was as a team, which sometimes required honest feedback. He slowly came to terms with the situation. He communicated back to his wife Maria that he needed to focus on what he was doing and nothing else. She understood and supported him, and soon he was in the right headspace.

When we finally reached our short-term goal at 87 degrees after our longest day yet on the ice, covering thirteen nautical miles, it was like a weight lifted off our shoulders. It was day forty of the expedition, and we still had 180 nautical miles to the North Pole, but at least we had reached the point where everything else was fading away back at home. Eric had reached what he likes to call his "day forty syndrome." That's where, miraculously, thoughts of home and everything else start to recede from your mind, and you go into survival mode, only focusing on the situation you are in now. We were coming into bigger pans of ice with less pressure ice between them, so we felt like we could have a glimmer of hope. To beat the speed record of forty-nine days, though, we would need to average twenty nautical miles a day—a feat that seemed completely unrealistic.

Fuel is everything on sea ice. Without it, we could not light the stoves to make water for drinking and hydrating our food. No water means death. It's that simple. Yet another calculation we had to manage was how much fuel we were using per day versus how much we had left to complete the journey. Those numbers were starting to not add up. Early in our trip, we had been using more fuel per day than we probably should have been, hedging our bets, lighting two stoves for part of each night and morning. One had been for melting and boiling water, and the other to warm the tent because it was so damn cold.

After some back-of-the-napkin calculations one evening, we figured we had to be more cognizant of our fuel use from here on out, or we would be dangerously low on fuel in the final push. Not only did we need those stoves for the skiing days, but we also had to have some leftover fuel in case of an emergency. We might be forced to sit out bad weather or wait for a weather window to open for the plane to come pluck us off the ice. It was frustrating, and I found myself doing maddening mental calculations on liters of fuel while skiing.

With limited days left to ski and a long way to go, we knew the only option left was to ski longer each day to gain more mileage. Obviously the more time on skis was important, as all progress stopped when we quit for the day. And we would lose distance while we ate and slept due to the drift.

We were already depleted of energy, mentally worn out, and physically beat up, yet we knew we had to adapt. Identifying a problem and fixing it was the name of the game on deteriorating sea ice as summer rapidly approached.

I was struggling with several small circles of red, painful skin on the back of both my thighs, which were getting worse. Commonly called "polar thigh," it often happens to the front of the legs where you are hit with cold wind for days on end. Mine was on the back of both my legs. For the life of me, I couldn't figure out if it was caused by not drying out enough at night or just good old wind and cold. Still, they were starting to be painful. I had experienced this on my skin during the Antarctica crossing, but those had been small and not very painful.

One night I had Eric use a pen to mark a circle around the edge of the worst of the two sores so that we could see any changes in the coming days. We noticed immediately that the sore on my left leg was growing with each day. At that point, I did not even care; we were too close now to making our goal, and besides, there was nothing I could do. I simply dried out my legs each night in the tent and put what remaining topical creams we had on the sores. The problem was that at night they were starting to get extremely painful. That was when I started to dive into our medical kit, not just for recreational purposes but for survival. The sore and surrounding large circle of red skin on my left leg throbbed so badly at night I couldn't sleep. Because the days were so taxing, sleep was the only good thing you had in your life, except maybe for food. Not to mention that since I wasn't sleeping well, I was getting more and more tired. So the painkillers we had with us were my only option. I started to take hydrocodone to ease the pain at night. It didn't help much, and I just had to deal with it. As the days dragged on, it started to get painful even while skiing, as my clothing layers would rub on the sores with each ski stride.

Since it was late April, we had one advantage that started to play in our favor: The sun was now rising higher in the sky and would never set. We had continual sunlight each day, which meant that skiing longer into the night was a possibility. Earlier in the trip, that had not been an option, since the sun did set and the temperature dropped so much it would have been dangerous to keep moving. But now, we could use the warmer temperatures and constant sun to our advantage.

On day forty-five of the expedition, we were 104 nautical miles away from the North Pole. We only had about five days of food left for each person. To say it was stressful would be an understatement. We did have our emergency rations, five days' worth for each person, in a special bag tucked at the bottom of the sleds. Still, we couldn't count on that food for travel in case an actual emergency happened. Skiing twenty nautical miles a day is a tall task on any polar expedition, but having already fought for forty-five days in the most difficult of environments made it even more unlikely.

The long ski days were taking their toll on us, but there was nothing to discuss or contemplate. We were in a daze, getting up each morning, doing the same routines burned into our minds. One particular day will stay with me forever. I was in the lead position, trying to navigate in a brutal whiteout. We had not been sleeping enough, and I was so tired that I literally could not stay awake while skiing. I was nodding off on my skis and trying everything to stay awake. I continually ran into huge blocks of ice without knowing they were there. At a break, thankful that Eric would now take over in the front, I almost melted down. I had been crying and generally having a fit inside my own little world. I told Eric at the break that I should write a country song titled "Crying in your Goggles" because that is what I had been doing. We both shared a moment, and then I passed off the lead. "Keep skiing" was all we repeated, out loud and in our heads.

We planned to hit some enormous pans of "milk and honey" ice once we hit the 88th parallel. Eric had told me about them from previous trips. We figured we would be able to fly to the finish line then. They had been well documented by explorers in the past, and the knowledge that they were out there had helped drive us forward in the hardest of times. The problem was that those big pans of ice were not materializing. Instead, with the warming late April spring temperatures, we were running into open water all the time. It was okay; we were prepared for open water. We had our dry suits to swim the leads, or we simply skied around them as necessary. But we were running into open leads everywhere; it was a nightmare. Some were thin leads that we could get across on our skis; some were partially frozen ones where we would get creative and raft our two sleds together and crawl across on top or pull each other across. The worst were the open leads as wide as fifty yards across that we had to swim. It was like a game of constant problem-solving.

The pans of ice were moving fast with the drift. There were times we could actually see ourselves moving as the ice pressured its way south. It was crazy. But our plan to attack the days with all we had was paying off. At one point, we averaged fifteen nautical miles a day for eight days in a row. I distinctly remember this period as one of the best stretches of weather possible. It was clear and relatively calm, which made all the difference. Instead of fighting through whiteout conditions where your forward progress might be halted by skiing into a block of ice without even knowing it, we could just head north. We had closed the gap, and though we had a long way to go and a short time to get there, the possibility of making it was under the surface. I cautioned myself not to get too confident, because there was always a good chance that something could come up and slow us down again.

On day forty-eight, we were seventy-one nautical miles from the Pole. The writing on the wall was clear—there would be no chance of breaking the speed record set by Cecilie, Rolf, and Per Henry, but that didn't matter anymore. Our goal was to make it through each day and reach the end. We had crossed the 89th parallel, and with 1 degree latitude of skiing left, any positive thoughts were tempered by the fact that our food supplies were dangerously low. We had sixty nautical miles remaining to reach the North Pole and two days of food left. To put that in context, that is a distance that typical commercial Last Degree trips (ski trips that cover the last sixty nautical miles to the Poles) will cover in seven or eight days.

We teetered on the edge. It would have been easy at this point just to say, "You know what, we made a great effort, but let's just camp and wait for the plane; at least we will have some food and fuel to fall back on." But Eric and I are not built that way. We had not arrived at this point in the Arctic by chance. The fight had been long and hard. Like a great blues guitar player, you need to have seen some shit and been through hard times to have the emotion to pour through your strings. We had both seen our share of shit on previous expeditions, as well as this one, and it was time to follow our souls. We realized we were not going to get any breaks.

Instead of folding, we rallied. We decided that the only way to go forward was to commit to the old Norwegian Viking mentality of a "Berserker run." We would go for it all, in a trance-like state that would not allow anything to stop us. We couldn't afford to sleep for a whole night anymore; the drift of the ice was causing too much backward distance. So we concocted a plan where we would ski for six hours and then put up the tent for a quick break. Resting and sleeping for a couple of hours would allow us to regain valuable energy but not lose much ground to drift. We developed a schedule of never having days and nights anymore. We would just ski for a set time, pause for a brief moment of rest, then hit it again.

We were so close to the Pole, but the surface was breaking up around us. Each day we were presented with countless small leads to navigate. We were running on empty. It could be two in the morning, and we would set up the tent, leaving most things in the sleds and just bringing in our sleeping system and the stoves to make water. We would lay down for a few hours and then pack up and be on the move again. It was now a race against time, and we didn't even know for sure anymore if we would make it. We just went forward; what little film and photos from this period are of two haggard and gaunt men struggling to finish their race with time.

On day fifty-two of the expedition, we were just sixteen nautical miles from the Pole. There was water everywhere. We would maneuver across snow bridges and small leads throughout the day, raft the sleds to save time, jump across cracks, anything to move forward. Every movement had only one purpose and nothing else. We moved as efficiently as possible, but the winds were strong, and the ice pans were drifting to the south at an alarming speed. If we stopped to read the GPS, we could see our position moving away from 90 degrees in real time on the screen. We were at the end of our rope.

We also were at the end of the time frame we had left to call for a pickup. The crew at Kenn Borek had already extended the time for us once; they would not do it again. It didn't matter to them if we were only one mile from our destination. It was all about safely landing on the ice and getting back out.

We went to sleep that night for a few hours and awoke on day fifty-three of the expedition with only three nautical miles left. We had no more energy in reserve, but we still got up early to make the final push for the end. We figured it should be an easy run since we were so close. The Arctic would have to give us good conditions, finally. We were wrong.

We came across yet another huge open-water lead. There were no breaks, not even at the end. We decided that Eric would swim it, and then I could simply ride on the two sleds rafted together; this would save time since both of us would not need to put on a dry suit.

Eric made it to the other side but couldn't find a way up onto the other side of the lead. It was terrifying. Over and over, he tried to pull himself over the edge of the ice but kept falling back into the water. Finally, he managed to get out on the other side, but the rope had fallen off his arm. He had to jump back into the water, find the rope, and repeat the process. When I finally got to the other side with the sleds, I was so happy he was okay. The two of us laughed at the insane situation and started skiing again.

It took us eight hours to cover the final three nautical miles. The unrelenting terrain and the southerly drift of the ice pack were a challenge until the bitter end. But as we walked the last meters to 90 degrees north latitude, the feeling was unlike anything I had ever experienced. Our small and scrappy team of two dedicated adventurers crossed the final steps together and stood at 90 degrees. It was a remarkable feeling.

We snapped a picture of the GPS and had no more steps to take. It was the best feeling in the world to put up our final tent and stop moving. We called the Kenn Borek flight team, notified them of our position, and promptly fell asleep for about ten hours. During the time we were sleeping, we drifted several miles in a southeasterly direction. We called back in to alert them of our new position, and there was a bit of tension as we learned that bad weather was approaching the area. This was quite nerve-racking because we had made an alarming inventory of our food. We had been forced to dip into our backup stash the last few days. If we could not get out soon, we possibly would have to wait out a five-day storm with roughly enough food for two days each. It was a grim thought. We wondered if fate still had it in for us.

Our contact at Kenn Borek called us back a bit later that day and told us the pilots had decided to beat the weather and had already taken off for Eureka. They would refuel and head our way. That was music to our ears, and we laid out brightly colored sacks of snow to mark the best line of potential landing on the big pan of ice we had happened to be on when we reached the top of the world.

Boarding that little Twin Otter airplane was terrific. The pilot wound up the engines and turned on the heat, and we opened the little packed lunches they had brought for us. It was like being in someone else's care, and we settled into the seats for the ride back to normalcy.

We had both completed what many people consider to be the most challenging expedition to accomplish. With the North Pole complete, I had finished an unlikely fourteen-year journey to climb the Seven Summits and ski unsupported/unassisted coast to North and South Pole trips. I felt a sense of pride and relief mixed together. The hardest of all the trips I had ever undertaken came at the end, and it took all the lessons I had learned along the way to make it. More importantly, I had shared both my polar trips with two of the best partners I could have ever dreamed of having. The lessons I learned on the Arctic Ocean, Antarctica, and traveling the world to climb its highest peaks will stay with me always.

Epilogue: Seven Years Onward

It is hard to believe that so much time has passed since our trip to the North Pole in 2014. We would be the last people to make that journey. The sea ice has continued to deteriorate at an alarming rate, and it is not feasible for anyone to make the trip from coast to Pole anymore. It saddens me that the opportunity for such an epic adventure as the one we had is now gone. My coast to North Pole trip also made me the last person to successfully join the True Adventurers Grand Slam club that way. Nowadays, people make a Last Degree trip instead.

With the end of our expedition, I had realized the culmination of an important personal and professional goal, one that took well over a decade of my life to complete. Due to the rigorous nature of the North Pole trip, it had a significant impact on me. Sitting in my seat of the Twin Otter as we headed south back to civilization, I was trying to wrap my head around what Eric and I had accomplished and the fact that I had achieved the Grand Slam. Though I wanted to reconnect with family and loved ones upon returning to the United States after the expedition, I knew I needed some time to process the journey.

After a quick turnaround of packing up our gear and getting organized back in Resolute, it was surreal to arrive back in Colorado. I knew that the arrival would be anticlimactic for me. While Eric would have Maria and Merritt (Eric's young son) waiting at Denver International Airport, no one would be there for me. When we walked into the main terminal, it felt good to be back in Colorado, and I gathered my bags like any other traveler and tossed them in the back of Eric's car. A bit disappointing, but it was nice to be back.

Maria and Eric graciously offered me a place to stay in their house. We made some jokes that I was already living there since I had decamped in their house the night before we left on the expedition. I thanked them for the offer, but I wanted to be alone for a few days. Mostly, I just wanted to relax and eat good food. I went to the Marriott in downtown Boulder, booked a room for three nights, and decompressed. It was exactly what I needed to do. I called friends and my parents and brother, but for the most part, I recuperated in the warm comfort of a room far away from the Arctic ice.

The issue of my former relationship still wasn't resolved after we got off the ice. I received messages of congratulations from Cecilie, but I didn't know where we stood. In the back of my mind, I thought that since my North Pole trip was over, I might be able to mend our broken bond. But I could sense that something was not the same as before, so I didn't push. Instead, I decided to go back to the life I had been living before heading north. She was living her life in Norway, and I was following mine on the other side of the Atlantic Ocean.

After resting for a few days, I had to figure out what was next since I had nothing pressing to do. Things were back to being easy: no more struggling to make water, skiing for twelve hours a day, or dodging polar bears. The act of simply going to a movie alone and eating popcorn in a warm theater was something I had been dreaming about for two months. After about a week, Eric and I met up to do something we had talked about for days on end on the ice: We had a cookout on his new deck with just a few friends, sipping good Colorado beers, devouring thick steaks, and swapping stories. It was amazing. You know the little things in life are important but take them for granted in normal times; they have more meaning when you miss them for so long.

The sore on my leg did, in fact, turn into frostbite. It was strange because it had only affected the surface layers of my skin, but it was large enough to cause a tremendous amount of pain. I will never forget the first shower I took when we got back to the mainland in Canada. I had to pull off the dry gauze pad that had now fused to my sore. I was screaming and crying out in the shower of an empty hotel. I had taped the pad onto the wound to cover it for the last five days of skiing since we had nothing else left to cover injuries with and it needed protection from rubbing. It was horrible. As soon as I got back to Colorado, I had a local dermatologist who dealt with cold injuries look at it. It was painful enough that he prescribed me some hard painkillers to take when I redid the dressings, which was an ordeal every time until it finally started to heal. I will never forget my friend Doug stopping by and commenting that he was concerned I was still taking hydrocodone for the pain. It's always good to have friends watching out for you.

I got an apartment in a quiet part of Boulder, slept a lot, and sipped gin and tonics in the summer sun on the patio. I even flew out to meet my brother Tate and some of his friends for a weekend in Las Vegas, weeping frostbite-injured leg and all, because why not? It was a bit of a celebratory time since I had pulled off the final piece of my big puzzle. But those feelings were tempered by a sadness just under the surface. I had made the Pole, but it had cost my relationship with Cecilie, one that had once been wonderful.

After more time passed, I started to drift back into work mode. I had a business to run, and things were coming back to life with clients for the future. I've always had a passion for helping clients that our company has developed strong bonds with over the years. Though I tried to get myself out of it, I guided our Denali trip that June to climb with some long-standing clients. It was a big mistake. I was fighting to keep my healing frostbite from getting worse and was too tired to be shoveling mountains of snow for three weeks on an arduous expedition. I talked it over with my co-guides and clients, and they agreed that I needed to go back to the real world and let my frostbite heal once and for all. I learned a good lesson about taking time to regain strength.

Over time I would hear from Cecilie that she had, in fact, decided to move on with her life. I can't blame her. There had been so many months of indecision and stalemate, mostly on my part, before I left Norway a year before. I expected it, but it was still devastating. After all the experiences we had shared, I was mostly mad at myself for messing it up. It took a lot of time, but I had no choice but to move on with my life. She was happy and had begun a relationship with Aleksander Gamme. The two would go on to have two daughters. I am sure she is an amazing mother. She has so much passion for the people she loves and is a truly giving person.

I focused on my business and continued to climb big mountains, which once again became my focus. I began traveling the usual guiding circuit, taking clients up the Seven Summits and other Himalayan peaks as a guide. One of the best outcomes from my many years of work was that I had built up a core group of clients from around the world that I loved. I have shared so many incredible journeys with them and still do.

The next significant relationship in my life started not too long after I completed the Grand Slam. It seems like another example of me being in the right place at the right time and following my gut instinct.

My best friend growing up was a guy named David Gauch. He lived across the street from me in Marietta, and he was my main camping buddy as we explored the woods and Soap Creek behind our neighborhood. I can attribute our time together as the beginning of my love for the outdoors, hiking, and camping. David went on to play football at the Air Force Academy, and once he was in the service, he was based at Laughlin Air Force Base in Del Rio, Texas. He met his future wife, Elsa, from the town just across the border, Acuña, Mexico. I went to their wedding when I was around twenty-two years old, which took place partly in Acuña and partly in Del Rio. It was quite the fiesta.

I had probably run across this cousin of Elsa's at the wedding, but I can't remember for sure, given that she was much younger. Regardless, when I saw a picture of Lorena Vazquez Morton at Elsa's younger brother's wedding some twenty years later, I was mesmerized. I asked Elsa about her cousin, and she suggested I reach out to Lore (short for Lorena). It seemed nuts, but since we were somewhat connected, I didn't think too much about it and sent her a text message. She was probably taken aback at first to get a text from some gringo out of nowhere. But with my good credentials being David's friend from childhood, she responded. We began to talk a lot, via texts at first and then on Skype. We got along quite well, and it was fun to learn about our different worlds, her living in Monterrey, Mexico, and me in Colorado.

That August I was guiding one of our Kilimanjaro climbs in Tanzania when I sent a message to Lore: "How about I come to visit for a coffee?" I think she was a bit surprised given the international distances, but that was something I was used to. It was not a big deal for me to fly to Mexico for a few days. She answered back, "You know I live in Monterrey, Mexico, not California, right?" We had a laugh, and not long after getting back to Colorado, I jumped a flight south.

Lore was recently divorced, and she had a two-year-old little girl named Sofia. We had such a great time the few days I was there. We kicked around her town and spent time at her parents' country house hanging out in the pool, and I met many of her friends. After about a month of back-and-forth conversations, we eased into a long-distance relationship.

Lore and I have been together since then, though there have been a few minor separations. The guide lifestyle is never easy on a relationship. It has been amazing to watch Sofia grow up; she is nine years old now. It's always fun to show them experiences that are more characteristic of Colorado, such as skiing, climbing, and trekking. Lore has been an amazingly supportive partner for a long time, bearing extended absences while I am in Pakistan or Antarctica for two months. She is an amazing woman.

Many of the same relationship challenges I have always faced still rear their ugly head occasionally, mostly revolving around my desire to always have another challenging project in some faraway mountain range. I still feel the pull in both directions: a great and stable "home life" balanced with wanting to go away for two months and climb an 8,000-meter peak in Tibet. It works somehow, primarily due to Lore's support and patience with this dirtbag mountain climber.

The time and effort I put into building Mountain Professionals began to pay off after I completed the Grand Slam as well. I have spent so many nights of my life on the side of a mountain or on a floating piece of polar ice, and have parlayed that experience into guiding those types of adventures. We regularly guide all the Seven Summits and Last Degree ski trips that cover the last sixty nautical miles to both the North and South Poles. I tend to guide the South Pole, and Eric guides our clients on the North Pole because I guide Everest during April, which is when the short North Pole trips take place. Eric continues to guide his own clients and works with sponsors doing speeches. He wrote a book about our North Pole trip together, with my co-author Hudson Lindenberger, called *On Thin Ice*. If you want a much deeper dive into our trip, I highly recommend it.

During the first week of January 2020, before the pandemic blew up, I received one of the worst calls of my life. I had just spent New Year's weekend with Lore and Sofia in Crested Butte, Colorado, with Eric, Maria, Merritt, and daughter Ellie, who had joined their family after our trip. Several of us had known Eric was not feeling so great for some time, but he didn't know exactly why. The day after we left their house, after skiing, cooking out, sharing cocktails, and watching football together, Eric had a colonoscopy. Around midweek, the results had come in.

When he called me, I could hear the shakiness in his voice right away. "Man, I have some bad news," he said, his voice trembling with tears. "I have colon cancer."

The news floored me. I sat on my deck in Boulder and tried to offer whatever assistance I could muster, which was nothing but words at that stage. Our close-knit group of friends in Colorado and an extensive network of friends and contacts from around the world rallied to support Eric and Maria and their family in any possible way, even if only with thoughts of support.

When Eric wrote his book, he had quite complimentary words for me as an expedition partner and called me his best friend. I feel the same way. He is someone I have shared experiences with that can't be described easily to other people. Along with Dave and Doug, he forms the circle of my closest pals, and we all know that we can rely on one another at the drop of a hat. All of our partners and families did the best we could to support the Larsen family during a treatment program that stretched over half a year since his diagnosis and still is ongoing. Through it all, Maria was exceptional and steadfast in taking care of their family.

As I write this, Eric is not out of the woods yet, though it looks promising that he will make a full recovery and return to his usual self. Hell, he is already riding challenging mountain bike trails and preparing for his next trip into the frozen north. I fully expect him to be taking clients on Last Degree trips and other polar expeditions for many decades to come. The guy is an inspiration to me and many other people around the world.

I have always thought of myself as a mountaineer first and foremost. Still, I didn't let my polar experience fall by the wayside. I went on to guide two more South Pole trips with clients. Each was unique. Both were entirely unsupported with no resupply drops. What can I say? I am a sucker for classic trips. The first one was a forty-four-day trip to the South Pole with three clients. On that expedition, we began at 82 degrees south latitude at the transition of the Ronne-Filchner Ice Shelf and the mainland, following the 1989 route to the Pole pioneered by Reinhold Messner and Arved Fuchs. The other was a fifty-three-day route from the more standard Hercules Inlet start.

I went on to receive my Master Polar Guide certification with the International Polar Guides Association. There are only thirteen Master Polar Guides in the world. I feel honored to be a part of that select group; many of these people were inspirational figures to me as I learned the intricacies of the polar environment.

This has put me in a unique position. I am one of the few guides that can lead people both to the summits of the highest mountains and to the most remote and harsh locations on the planet at the Poles. I love both, but the mountains will always be my first love. At present, I have successfully guided clients on the Seven Summits so many times I've lost count. Still, there is one in particular that has captured my heart, Aconcagua, the first of the Seven Summits I ever climbed. I have stood atop her more than twenty-five times now, though my memories of specific climbs have somewhat blurred, perhaps due to the ample Malbec and steaks we indulge in after coming down.

I have been fortunate to summit Everest six times so far. Who would have thought that a kid who grew up focused on football in Georgia would one day be able to say that? I plan to guide that trip for several more years before handing off the reins to another of our guides to lead. At some point, I will be the old-school expedition leader who manages things from base camp and lets the youngsters have their fun up high. But that day is still some years off in the future!

As for the 8,000-meter mountains, I am still chasing them. I have participated in or led twenty-one expeditions up those magnificent mountains and have managed to summit fourteen times on five different ones—Everest six times, Manaslu three times, Lhotse and Cho Oyu twice, and Broad Peak once. I have fond memories of the summits I've missed, too. Knowing when to turn around is a valuable skill to have when partaking in any climbing, not just high-altitude adventures. Besides turning back on Dhaulagiri during the season with Cecilie, I had two expeditions on Everest where I did not make the summit. One was the earthquake season in 2015 when the mountain closed due to the avalanche. Another was in 2005 when I developed a nasty chest infection as we were on the summit push. I came close on a Gasherbrum 2 trip, but it ended with a mighty avalanche and subsequent rescue scenario. Plus, there was my trip to K2 and one to Broad Peak, when the conditions for a safe summit never materialized.

The idea of trying for all fourteen 8,000-meter peaks, which used to dominate in my mid-thirties, has waned in recent years, mainly due to focusing on my business and my relationship. But it is always there, lingering in the subconscious. We shall see what the future holds.

I find myself looking at sailboats often. The dream of sailing around the world is still a tempting goal. I was pretty close to taking the leap and buying a sailboat of my own, but the events of 2020 put a delay in that plan. When we canceled our Mountain Professionals 2020 Everest expedition due to COVID-19, I, along with many others, figured it would be a quick rebound and a summer full of work. We had been scheduled to have by far the biggest revenue year in our fifteen-year history. The global pandemic, which caused many others a lot more emotional hardship through sickness and deaths in their families, caused a substantial financial strain on a business like ours. For all intents and purposes, we were out of business for over a year, and I was basically unemployed and fronting the company's operating costs. It did give me time to write this book, though, so it was not a complete washout.

We are slowly getting back to work, and I am confident that people's desire to go on adventures will only be more robust. The virus continues to persist, and the near-term future presents challenges, but I have faced many challenges on the ice and in the mountains. They have taught me that a little problem-solving and a self-reliant spirit will get me through anything the world can throw at me. Mountain Professionals will survive and thrive.

The lessons I have learned along the way, the teamwork and people I have shared successes and failures with, and the joyous times I have experienced in the outdoors are what continue to drive me to this day. It might be unlikely that I keep pushing and climb all the remaining 8,000-meter mountains I have on my tick list or sail around the world, but who knows? It was damn unlikely that I should have ever climbed the Seven Summits and skied to the North and South Poles, yet I did all that in the most unlikely manner. Let us wait and see. I do know one thing: I will never stop chasing my dreams.

Index

ABOUT THE AUTHORS

Ryan Waters is a professional mountaineer, mountain guide, and polar adventurer. He has worked in the professional guiding and outdoor education field for eighteen years. His expeditions have taken him to Nepal, Argentina, Chile, Ecuador, Tibet, Pakistan, Mexico, Russia, Tanzania, Greenland, Indonesia, Antarctica, the Arctic Ocean, and beyond. His guiding résumé includes over fifty ascents of the various Seven Summits, well over thirty-five expeditions in the Andes Range, and twenty-four expeditions to the Himalayas including six summits of Everest and fourteen times standing on the summit of various 8,000-meter mountains. A team unsupported west-to-east ski traverse of Greenland expanded his interests into the polar regions, where he cut his teeth on difficult polar ski expeditions in addition to climbing. In 2010, Ryan and Cecilie Skog completed a 1,120-mile Antarctica ski expedition over seventy days from Berkner Island in the Ronne-Filchner Sea to the South Pole, continuing to the Ross Sea to complete the first ski traverse of Antarctica without resupplies or the use of kites. In 2014, Ryan and Eric Larsen skied for fifty-three days to complete the last unsupported full ski expedition to the North Pole. The expedition was made into a two-hour Discovery Channel documentary. He has contributed as a writer to several media outlets, books, and documentaries, including the book *Antarctica*, published in Norway by Gyldendal. His photographs have been published in several magazines, books, gear catalogs, web outlets, and two book covers. He has a Bachelor of Science degree in geology and is a certified Master Polar Guide with the International Polar Guides Association.

Hudson Lindenberger is a full-time, award-winning journalist and author whose work has appeared in *Men's Journal*, *Backpacker*, *5280*, and

y other regional and national publications. He was co-author of *On*
Ice: An Epic Final Quest into the Melting Arctic, which told the story
Eric Larsen and Ryan Waters's trip to the North Pole, a gold medalist
he 21st Annual Independent Publisher Book Awards. When Linden-
rger is not writing, he spends his time in the mountains of Colorado
king, biking, and climbing.